THE LEADERSHIP WAY

Management
For The Nineties

**How To Get Top Results
In Managing and Supervising People**

John D. Peyton, Ph.D.

Davidson Manors, Inc., Publishers
Valparaiso, Indiana

DMI
DAVIDSON MANORS, INC., PUBLISHERS
P.O. Box 548, Valparaiso, IN 46384

THE LEADERSHIP WAY, Management for the Nineties:
How to Get Top Results in Managing and Supervising People

Printed in the United States of America.
Library of Congress Catalog Card Number 91-60774

Publisher's Cataloging-In-Publication Data:

Peyton, John D.
The Leadership Way, Management for the Nineties:
    How to Get Top Results in Managing and Supervising People
Includes index.
    1.   Leadership.
    2.   Management.   I. Title.
HD57.7   1991   658.4'092   91-60774

ISBN   0-9628901-5-4

CONTENTS

ABOUT THE AUTHOR

John Peyton has a unique combination of academic and business experience.

He holds a B.A. degree from Oberlin College and M.A., M.S., and Ph.D. degrees from the University of Pittsburgh. He was a Woodrow Wilson Fellow, Andrew Mellon Fellow and University Fellow at Pittsburgh, and a Postdoctoral Fellow at The Center for Advanced Study in Theoretical Psychology, University of Alberta.

He has taught at the University of Missouri, University of Alberta, College of Wooster and Valparaiso University. Administrative positions held include Director of Continuing Education at the College of Wooster, and Director of The Program for the Support of Business and Industry at Valparaiso University.

Dr. Peyton has also been a corporation manager, real estate broker and management consultant. He has over nineteen years experience in conducting management courses and seminars. Clients have included some of the largest U.S. corporations, many small and medium-sized companies, government agencies, law-enforcement groups, university administrations, school systems, hospitals and health care facilities.

Dr. Peyton is now president of a real estate investment and property management company. He continues to teach and consult.

ACKNOWLEDGEMENTS

This book would have been impossible without the assistance of many people, including Ralph Hazlett, whose collaboration started the project many years ago; Gale Corley, who encouraged me to put it in writing; Joyce Hicks, Ellen Corley, Ralph Joseph, Curt Gill, William Anderson and Lucinda Ruge, whose comments surely improved the result; Evelyn Gray, who typed the first drafts; the many students who have participated in my seminars; and Sue Peyton, my wife, who has advised me, encouraged me and patiently endured the writing of the book for so long.

The book is dedicated to Sue.

DISCLAIMER

Warning: The purpose of this book is to provide information. It is sold with the understanding that the author and publisher are not engaged in giving legal, psychological or other expert advice. If such advice is required, readers should consult a competent professional.

A great deal of care has gone into the preparation of this work. Even so, there may be mistakes. The book should be used as a general guide and not the final answer to management or leadership questions. Indeed, the message of the work is that there are no easy or simple answers for such problems. Every situation must be evaluated individually and decisions to act made with careful consideration of all relevant facts and circumstances.

The author and publisher have no liability to any person or organization for any actual or alleged loss from information in this book. Any purchaser unwilling to accept the above conditions may return the book to the publisher for a full refund.

STEP ONE

UNDERSTANDING THE ROLE OF A LEADER

CHAPTER 1

INTRODUCTION

The best managers have always been leaders — people who could inspire and motivate employees, knew how to gain and give cooperation, were good communicators, won the confidence of others and could work with people without conflict. Because they had good leadership skills, they got results.

Now, all managers will need these skills. One reason for this is the changing labor force. People of different cultural, ethnic and educational backgrounds are now working together; employees' values and expectations are changing; there is evidence that the "work ethic" is weakening; some workers are not prepared academically; there is little organizational loyalty, especially when working conditions are poor or opportunity appears elsewhere. Furthermore, employees today do not want to be managed in the old ways. They want their managers and supervisors to be people they can respect and want to follow, that is, leaders.

Competition is another factor forcing change. Organizations managed in The Leadership Way are more efficient and productive. These companies will drive the poor performers out of business. Similar financial pressures are bearing on all organizations — including government and the nonprofits — to improve performance, increase quality and accomplish more for less money.

These challenges can only be met with better management leadership, at all levels.

The Leadership Way shows how to manage by leadership. It is designed to develop the leadership ability of each individual manager and supervisor, and to be applied throughout the organization.

The methods are practical, straight forward and "common sense." They can be used by chief executive officers, first-line supervisors, managers of all kinds, group leaders, professionals and independent business people, in profit and nonprofit organizations and large or small companies.

The book is divided into three "steps," corresponding to stages of understanding and development of abilities. Since each topic builds on the preceding ones, it is best to read the chapters in order. Later, the book can be used for reference and as a guide in handling specific situations.

CHAPTER 2

THE CHARACTERISTICS
OF EFFECTIVE LEADERS

Leaders come in all shapes and sizes.

Some are tall (George Washington) and some are small (Napoleon). Some are kind and considerate (Jesus); some are merciless dictators (Alexander the Great, Hitler). Some are dashing and colorful (George Custer, George Patton), and some are not (Ghandi, Harry Truman).

Some are rich and some poor; some are educated, some uneducated; some are well-liked, some are well-hated; some are intelligent, some are stupid, and some are probably insane.

It seems that for any characteristic you can imagine, you can find many leaders who had it and many who did not.

Hundreds of research studies have been conducted to find out if there are any personal characteristics common to all leaders. The results have been disappointing. The only consistent findings are that leaders are usually

- taller,
- more intelligent, and
- have more energy

than others in their group.

Other factors have less to do with personal characteristics and more to do with circumstances. For example, leaders often have one or more strong supporters in the group.

Since it is obvious that people must have some traits that cause them to be leaders, later research sought to identify which personal characteristics might be most important in varying circumstances. This approach was more fruitful. "Contingency," "managerial grid," "leadership style," and "situational leadership" theories emerged from its findings. It showed that different types of leaders are more effective for different types of people, kinds of work, power positions of the leader and leader popularity. The leader's motivation was also found to be important.

Most recently, studies have focused on the functions of leadership, that is, what leaders *do* in and for their organizations. The results are useful because they identify leadership behaviors which can be learned and can be developed in others.

Among the most important of the leadership functions are the following.

Key Functions Of Leaders:

The effective leader provides a vision for the organization.

The leader has thought about what the organization could be and could accomplish. The leader is very clear about what he or she wants it to become. The leader's vision (mission) for the organization goes far beyond the day-to-day setting of objectives and solving of problems. It must be both grand enough to be inspiring and practical enough to be believed.

The effective leader communicates the organizational vision in such a way that it inspires a following and motivates people to action.

There is a secret to doing this successfully: the leader himself must believe passionately in the vision. Only then can he* convince others what a wonderful thing it would be for the organization to develop in this direction. He shows each person involved how he or she will benefit, both in satisfaction of the individual's wants and goals, and because the significance of the organizational achievement will add meaning to that person's work and life.

The leader exercises initiative and assumes responsibility.

Many people are leaders of groups solely because they had the initiative to organize the group or start the

---

*   "He" and "she" (and "him" and "her") are interchangeable
      in this book. The principles apply equally to both sexes. Use
      of the different pronouns is purely stylistic.

13

project. This gives them a right to lead in the eyes of the others. Leaders also voluntarily assume responsibility for obtaining the desired results. Initiative and responsibility are two of the major functions a group expects of its leader.

This is especially true in smaller, face-to-face groups. The leader who does not work harder than others may retain the title of leader, but the group is actually led by someone else or by no one at all. The type of work a leader does is often quite different from that of others in the group, so the difficulty of tasks may not be directly comparable. Still, the members will have a pretty good idea of how much the leader is doing. It is the impression gained by the group that is most important.

The leader thinks and plans for the group as a whole. The leader often solves problems for the group.

People look to the leader for decisions, plans and solutions on the broadest and most far-reaching concerns facing the group. On more specific issues, the leader may or may not make the decisions. Sub-group leaders usually plan, make decisions, and solve problems for their part of the organization. Often, people neither expect nor welcome the overall leader's participation at this level.

The leader is highly goal-oriented, self-motivated and self-disciplined.

It is partly for these reasons that she initiates projects, works hardest, and cares deeply about her organizational vision. Self-direction and self-motivation are generally regarded as difficult. Having these abilities wins the respect of others and justifies the position of the leader.

The leader sets an example for others, personifies the ideal for the group and expresses the values of the organization.

A leader sets an example whether she wants to or not. People will look to her character and behavior, even more than her words, to decide how they should act. People want their leaders to be admirable.

The leader possesses knowledge, skills, characteristics or resources which are valuable to the group and needed for its success.

For example, a political leader may have the ability to get votes. A business leader may have the technical knowledge needed to design the product, the managerial skills needed to organize the work, or the money needed to start the company.

A person may be a leader at one time and not another. At the scene of an accident, a doctor or paramedic becomes an instant leader because his knowledge and skills are those most needed. At a fire, the fire captain becomes a leader. In times of crisis, we may choose a strong, directive leader; in quieter times, we may elect a non-directive type of leader who will share control and allow others to participate in the decision-making process.

The leader possesses leadership skills.

Once in a position of leadership, a person must maintain that position through successful performance. This includes the ability to work effectively with others.

The leader wins the trust and respect of the group.

As a leader, your basic motives, attitudes toward others and general methods of dealing with people are of crucial importance in determining your acceptance.

The next chapter provides initial guidelines for developing the motives and methods you will need.

CHAPTER 3

HOW YOU CAN BECOME A SUCCESSFUL LEADER AND MANAGER

Be a Leader, not a Boss.

A Boss has attitudes that imply,

"I don't care what you think, we are going to do it my way!"

"Never mind what you want, do what I tell you!"

"What I think and want is the only important consideration; what you think or want does not matter."

"If necessary, I will force you to do what I say!"

A Boss is the type of manager who thinks only of himself, with no regard for what other people may want or believe. A Boss usually does not even consider any desires or opinions but his own.

The primary methods of a Boss are
- giving orders,
- invoking authority, demanding obedience, using overt and implied threats,
- exercising the power to reward and punish, and
- utilizing various forms of personal pressure, such as intimidation, ridicule, venting anger and being overbearing.

Being a Boss is very tempting for two types of managers: those who are obsessed with immediate results and those who enjoy wielding power over other people. Another attraction of authoritarianism is that, when it works, it is quick and effective. If there is no resistance or resentment from others, a Boss can achieve results with great efficiency.

Some people can tolerate Bosses better than others. Those who were in military service for a long time, come from a family with authoritarian parents, or who feel secure in a highly-structured environment may actually prefer an autocratic manager.

However, most people dislike working for a Boss, especially in countries where democracy and individualism are cultural ideals.

Employees of a disliked Boss will
- resist the Boss by actively fighting back or passively refusing to do what he wants,
- resent him and find ways to get revenge,
- avoid him whenever possible;
- escape completely by finding employment elsewhere.

Even when employees will accept such treatment, there are serious disadvantages to being a Boss. Employees are usually less motivated under autocratic management and do not perform very well. Further-more, people who are always told what to do will lose their ability to think and act on their own. The Boss then has a less capable work force. He cannot go anywhere or do anything different because his employees are depend-ent on him for constant direction. He will also miss new ideas and the intellectual stimulation that comes from people of differing opinions and points of view.

The worldwide success of non-autocratic manage-ment styles is proving that "The Boss" is obsolete and comparatively ineffective.

Be a Leader, not a Manipulator.

A Manipulator thinks

"I want to get something for nothing from these people."

"I want to set things up so that I will be sure to come out ahead."

"I will find a way to take advantage of them and trick them into doing what I want."

A Manipulator gets others to act by making them believe, falsely, that they will receive certain benefits in return. Manipulators are frequently very attractive and charming people. These traits help them to be successful.

Like a Boss, a Manipulator does not care about anyone but herself. Unlike a Boss, a Manipulator *does* think about what others want, but she does this only to trick them. She believes that fooling people is easier than forcing them.

The primary method used by a Manipulator is making false predictions and promises. These may be stated boldly, conveyed by implication, or created by the with-holding of essential information.

Amazingly, many Manipulators are proud of their methods. They think of their victims as "suckers," who deserve to be cheated because they are "stupid enough" to believe the Manipulator's lies. By this twisted logic, the Manipulator becomes a sort of hero in his or her own eyes.

Those who recognize a Manipulator for what she is can work with her by protecting themselves, but they must always be on guard against some new trick.

When others realize how they have been harmed by a Manipulator, they will seek revenge. They will resist any future activities of the Manipulator and will try to get rid of or escape from her.

For these reasons, manipulation works best in short-term relationships. Even there, the reputation of the Manipulator may spread, warning off future victims.

Another disadvantage of deception — for those who care about such things — is the terrible self-opinion the Manipulator must have, namely, as a person who can never succeed except by being dishonest.

To be a real Leader, find ways to help others in return for the help they give you.

A true Leader asks himself,

"How can I benefit others at the same time I am benefitting myself?"

"What can I do to solve the group's problem or make the outcome better for all?"

"How can I give all involved something they want?"

A real Leader does not use force or deception. He or she uses persuasion to gain cooperation. People follow a leader because they see a way to gain something they want by doing so.

The particular benefits received from a Leader can vary as much as the different wants of individuals and the different purposes of groups. For example, a scientific leader may provide new discoveries and inventions; a political leader may inaugurate a better social order; a business leader may create new jobs and better, cheaper products.

Because a Leader does not resort to force or deception, he does not have to contend with the problems created by those methods. People do not resist, resent or try to escape from someone who is helping them achieve their goals. Leadership utilizes *positive incentive*, a very powerful motivator. It releases people's potential to work, produce, create and succeed.

In return, the Leader receives the benefits of
- accomplishing more than he could achieve alone, for the organization, other people, and his own advancement;
- working effectively with others, being liked and admired, gaining a good reputation and a positive self-image;
- the avoidance of unnecessary problems and hassles;
- enjoying a significant competitive advantage over groups headed by Bosses and Manipulators.

To become an effective Leader/Manager, start by observing

The Fundamental Rules of Leadership:

1. Find or create mutually-beneficial objectives and projects;
2. Provide benefits to others in return for their contributions to the success of the group;

3. Develop systems that create conditions needed for group effectiveness;

4. Solve problems by making sure that each person receives something he or she wants;

5. Develop your leadership skills.

In addition to the above, you will need to meet these two

Key Leadership Objectives:

First, you must achieve the goals of the organization. You must obtain the needed performance from your employees and production from your section. Without adequate performance, the organization will fail and everyone will suffer. A Leader finds ways to reach objectives if at all possible, even in the face of inadequate resources, employees who do not want to do the work, or other significant difficulties.

Second, you must help those who work with you to achieve some of their goals. The benefits you provide must be fair compensation for the work they have done. It may be difficult to provide adequate rewards for all, especially if you lack sufficient funding or there are factors working against a fair distribution system. Still, people must benefit appropriately; otherwise, they will not perform adequately or will leave, and, again, the organization will fail.

Both of these key objectives — achieving satisfactory performance and providing adequate rewards — are the responsibility of the Leader.

Managers practicing Leadership for the first time may have to make some adjustments in their own behavior. You may be naturally more task-oriented or more people-oriented. As a Leader, you must pursue both goals.

A Leader must also learn to resist the natural human inclination to think exclusively about what he wants. When you are in a position of leadership, you are expected to think first about the wants of others. You must seek out goals and formulate plans that will benefit the group.

On the other hand, you must still insist on performance from others. If you are reluctant to confront people on difficult matters, you will have to find a way to overcome your reluctance. Management cannot be a "charity program," where people receive but do not perform.

In the upcoming chapters, you will learn specific methods to use in achieving the objectives of management leadership. The first two chapters are the most theoretical. They must be covered first because they lay the foundation for all that follows. Be sure to read them before proceeding to the rest.

At the end of each topic are examples and practice cases. These will help you apply the principles to real situations. If you faithfully practice the methods described, they will become easy and automatic.

Think about the ideas as you read. Ask yourself questions such as these:

"Does this make sense to me?"

"Does this fit my experience?"

"Have I encountered similar situations and problems?"

Then, challenge yourself to apply the material by asking,

"How is this point illustrated in my work or organization?"

"How could I use this principle to improve my performance?"

"How could we make use of these methods in our company?"

"What difficulties might we encounter in applying this material and how could they be overcome?"

Finally, ask yourself,

"Have I made a *definite commitment* to improve my leadership ability and become a more effective manager?"

To a large extent, *your success depends upon your answer*.

SUMMARY

A real Leader has a vision for the organization, communicates this vision to others, inspires and motivates. A Leader exercises initiative, assumes responsibility, works hardest, thinks and plans. A Leader is highly motivated, goal-oriented and self-disciplined. A Leader sets an example and personifies group values. A Leader has knowledge, skills or resources needed by the group. A Leader exercises leadership skills and is trusted and respected by others.

A Leader is not a Boss who has no regard for people, uses force and creates resistance; nor is a Leader a Manipulator who only pretends to care about what others want, uses deception and gains people's resentment and revenge.

A true Leader helps other people get what they want in return for their help in achieving group goals. A Leader fulfills both functions of leadership: achieving the organization's objectives and benefitting those who help.

STEP TWO

DEVELOPING
LEADERSHIP ABILITY

CHAPTER 4

GAINING A PRACTICAL UNDERSTANDING OF PEOPLE

Thinking of others in terms of your own wants and expectations is a natural human tendency. You want others to do things which will benefit you. You expect them to obey the rules of conduct which you accept. You often expect certain actions from others solely because you think they "ought to" behave this way.

Unfortunately for this type of thinking, other people are not governed to any great extent by your desires or your opinions of right and wrong. If you are to understand people in a way that is both practical and realistic, you must understand the *actual causes* of their thinking and behavior.

The causes of human actions are those combinations of conditions and events that bring them about. We assume that every occurrence has a cause, even if we do not know what it is. That cause is to be found in the events and conditions existing just before and at the same time as the occurrence.

Although each occurrence in the universe is unique, and has its own unique set of conditions that causes it, similar events (kinds of events) are usually caused by the same kinds of conditions. Whenever we discover a connection between kinds of conditions and subsequent occurrences, we say we have found a *causal law*. For example, when certain types of material are heated in the presence of oxygen, a fire always results. From this fact comes a causal law: the combination of fuel, heat and oxygen at a particular time and place causes (brings about) fire.

Causal laws can be very useful, as this example illustrates. If you want a fire, the law tells you how to get one — create the proper causal conditions. If you do not want a fire, this law tells you how to prevent it — eliminate the conditions that would cause it.

Are there causal laws for human behavior? Yes, although the causes of human actions and reactions are considerably more complex than those for fire. Let us examine some of the causes which typically produce people's thoughts, feelings and actions.

Actions come from feelings.

The immediate cause of human actions is feelings, also called emotions or inner-urges. We act as we do because, at that time and place, that action is what we most *feel* like doing. These feelings can take various forms, including impulses, volitions and what is called "will power" or "determination."

Sometimes we think we are acting against our strongest feelings. This is because we are resisting those feelings that would normally cause us to do some other action. We are most aware of them because we are working against them. However, we always act in line with our *strongest* impulses.

Here are some examples of feelings and the actions they cause:

- Starting a fight, caused by anger;
- Quitting, caused by discouragement or fatigue;
- Buying something, caused by desire;
- Acting purposefully, caused by a volition based on an earlier decision to act.

The practicality of this rule, that feelings cause actions, is easily illustrated. For example, you might want a person to perform his job carefully and well and wonder what could cause him to do so. You would look to feelings for possible effective causes, such as the feeling of *enjoyment* in doing good work, *pride* in performance, *desire* for the rewards, *fear* of being fired, a sense of *duty* or a feeling of *responsibility*.

If you want *your* people to work carefully and well, consider which of these causes (feelings) would work best in your situation. Ask yourself, "How could I create a feeling of job responsibility in my employees?" or "How could I make doing good work more enjoyable?" Keep looking until you find the causes that will work for you.

Sometimes, feelings which bring about the results you want also create effects you do not want. For instance, fear of being criticized could make employees work harder, but also make them hate their jobs. If this happened, they would quit at the first opportunity to take a position elsewhere. The resulting high employee turnover could more than offset any positive effects.

As a leader, you should seek out those causal conditions which have the best overall results and are within your power to create.

Feelings come from beliefs.

The feelings, emotions and inner urges that lead to action are caused by a person's beliefs, combined with his wants, habits, personality and thinking. The immediate cause of feeling is when a person comes to believe that something is true or thinks of it as true. (Physical conditions in the body can also influence feelings.)

Some examples of beliefs causing feelings are these:
- *Anger* caused by the belief that someone has done something to you that you dislike and believe he had no right to do.
- *Fear* caused by the belief, "I am in danger."
- *Discouragement* caused by the belief, "I cannot do this."
- *Volition to act* caused by the decision, "I will do it now."

To return to our earlier example, how could you create a feeling of job responsibility in employees? You would succeed if they came to believe, "I should do my work well; the best thing for me to do is to produce the desired results." Thus, when a person voluntarily assumes a responsibility, he says to himself, "This is something I will do or will see that it is done."

We use the word *responsibility* in two ways. In the first, we employ rules for judging what "ought" to have hap-

29

pened. If we can say, "You ought to have done this," then we can hold you responsible for the consequences of not doing it. This first sense of responsibility is often retributory: we use it to blame and punish misbehavior. The second sense of *responsibility* is not concerned with fixing blame or with what "ought" to be done. It is contained in the decision that the person makes when he or she says, "I will see to it that the desired result is obtained." By deciding, "I will do this," and determining to carry through on that decision, the person *is* assuming responsibility in the active sense of the word. That is the sense we want. It gets the results.

Beliefs influence our feelings even when we are not consciously thinking about them. The more strongly we hold an opinion and the more we care about the matter, the greater is its power to influence our feelings and our actions.

Beliefs come from thinking.

People come to believe as a result of their thinking. They cognitively process information (think) and either accept or reject conclusions drawn from that information.

The thinking process is not always conscious. We may be unable to say why we believe what we do. Some beliefs, such as those involved in perception, seem to be automatic. Research suggests that these are actually the result of highly-complex processes of subconscious information reception and identification, analogous to hypothesis testing in science.

We often abbreviate our thinking or recall conclusions reached in earlier thought, rather than think through a matter step-by-step each time it arises. Like everything else, thinking can become habitual.

Here is an example of a line of thought which leads to the belief, "I should do my work carefully and well and make sure the results turn out right."

- "The work I do here at the hospital is very important for the welfare of the patients."
- "I want to help other people, as well as myself. It makes me feel good and I believe everyone should help others."
- "I like my job here and want to keep it. This requires me to do good quality work."
- "I can do this work well, if I try."
- "Therefore, the best thing for me is to do my job carefully and well and make sure it turns out right."
- "That is what I will do."

Of course, the person may still fail to perform well. It may be beyond her ability, outside factors may prevent it, she may change her mind, or her decisions may have little effect on her behavior (low will power or mental problems can cause this).

Even so, the manager who stimulates these beliefs and decisions has a much better chance of obtaining good quality work than one who just declares that employees "ought to" do their jobs properly.

This is only one example. There are other lines of thought which could lead to the feeling of job responsibility. There are other feelings which could cause a person to do good work. As managers, we must not assume that there is only one way to accomplish something. Different occasions and different people will call for different methods. What worked or failed once may not again.

There are no *simple* rules that will always guarantee good results in working with people. If you care about

the goals you are pursuing, you will not give up if one method fails. You will keep trying different methods (causes) until you find one that succeeds.

Thinking comes from wants and experience.

People *think about* what they want; they *think with* information and skills gained from their experience.

To a certain extent, we think about everything that gets our attention. We also think in seemingly random chains of ideas, as in daydreaming. We may think about a topic merely because we enjoy thinking about it, or because of a general desire to know (curiosity).

However, thought which is sustained and leads to action is determined mostly by our wants. Our wants cause us to think about things which might satisfy those wants. Thus, wants provide the subject-matter for much of our thought.

The content of our thought — ideas, concepts and beliefs — comes from our experience. You cannot think about something unless you have experienced it in some way. For example, you can not think about, "What should I feed a Wandering Squigglefoos?" if you have never seen or even heard of such an animal. Of course, you can think about the name of the beast, which you have just experienced by reading it.

A farmer thinks about the weather; an investor thinks about the stock market; a child thinks about escaping from her homework and going to play; a lover thinks about his beloved. The connection with wants is obvious in each case.

If thinking is determined by a person's wants and experience, can these facts be applied to management? Yes, there are several important implications for managers.

First, do not expect new employees or those without sufficient background *to be able to* think effectively for themselves. Beginners need to be directed until they have learned enough, through training and experience, to think independently. Ability to solve practical problems is directly related to *specific knowledge* of the job or subject.

Second, do not expect people *to want to* think constructively about a matter if they see no connection between the subject and any of their wants. Tell them how the matter you wish to discuss is connected with some goal which they value. Then they will be able to say to themselves, "This is important to me; it is a way toward my goals," instead of thinking, "Why is he asking me about this? How can I get out of here?"

Earlier we saw how thinking in certain ways could lead to a feeling of job responsibility. We now see why such reasoning may fail to occur. It will not happen if the person does not care about helping others or doing a good job. In that case, he or she will think about other things or will arrive at different conclusions.

Wants come from experience, plus inborn needs.

People's wants are caused by two factors: experience and inborn processes.

We do *not* learn to want food or rest: these are inborn wants, caused directly by physical conditions in the body.

We *do* learn to want sports cars, nice clothes, good friends and more education.

The mechanism by which wants are acquired is described by

The Law of Effect:

> If you experience something which you like, you will want it again in the future. Thus, you will tend to repeat those behaviors that lead to positive results.
>
> If you experience something which you do not like, you will want to avoid it in the future. Thus, you will tend to avoid behaviors that lead to negative results.

Many of our motives are formed by combinations of inborn processes and experience. You may be hungry for purely physical reasons, but you are hungry for a double-decker hamburger because of your previous positive experiences with them.

Even psychologists frequently have difficulty un-ravelling the complex combinations of motives which underlie much of our behavior. Luckily, we need not know exactly *why* people want what they do. We can work with them if we can know or guess *what* they want.

Part of raising children, in any society, involves a process called *socialization*. This is the program of training and experience which causes them to want to perform socially-useful instead of socially-destructive behaviors. These motives are too important for our society to be left to chance. We create them deliberately, by providing appropriate rewards and punishments over a long period of time. As a result, most people are motivated to do the "right" thing in most instances, the "right" thing being that which will benefit their immediate group in particular and other people in general.

Because of socialization, we can assume that many people will want to help others besides themselves and do the "right" things. We depend on these general motives when we seek to instill a feeling of responsibility or appeal to a sense of fair play.

A person who has not been socialized is very hard to manage. In such cases, we can motivate only through direct, personal rewards and punishments. Individual consequences must be carefully monitored because the person will never respond to the good of others or to group goals.

One can go too far the other way, of course. A person may care too much for others' needs and too little for his own, or want to give more than is reasonable for the rewards provided. Others in the group may resent this individual because they think he is trying to make them look bad, and the manager will have trouble balancing his performance with appropriate rewards. Although it is tempting to take advantage of such persons, the leader should not do so. He should either increase their rewards or reduce their self-sacrificing behavior.

Experience comes from inner responses.

Experience consists of the sum of a person's inner reactions to occurrences, especially those which have come into his attention.

Experience is not what happens to someone; it is how he or she responds to what happens. The nature of an experience is determined by the types of inner responses which comprise it.

For example, if two people are thrown into the water from a boat and both make it to shore safely, you might be tempted to say that they had the same experience. This is not necessarily true. One might have been a good swimmer who was not worried at any time. The other may have been terrified. Or, one might have been trying to murder the other by drowning him. For the would-be murderer, the experience was a disappointment; for the other, it was a relief.

A worker with ten years experience is more effective than a new employee because of the valuable work-related reactions he has accumulated. These could include increased knowledge of the job, increased ability to solve problems and innovate, improved skills, greater reliability, and a greater consistency of performance.

The value of additional experience ends when a worker ceases to improve as a result. It is sometimes said that such an individual does not have ten years experience, but only one year of experience which has been repeated nine times. In other words, this worker stopped learning and improving his skills, which are the relevant reactions to being on the job, nine years ago.

Experience includes all of a person's present awareness and all memories, learned responses, skills and habits.

Inner responses come from attention.

Attention is the first cognitive response to a stimulus. An occurrence of which we are totally unaware will not enter into our thoughts at all. We will not react to it if it does not reach us through our attention.

We may respond to subconscious stimuli, but the extent of these influences is not great. Our experience can be affected by purely physical factors such as the chemical composition of our blood and our brain functioning. We may respond to our own subconscious information processing. However, none of these influences is easily modified by either the person having them or by anyone else.

From a practical viewpoint, a manager can best influence a person's experience by providing occurrences which come into his attention and to which he reacts in a useful way. A new employee should be given training which brings important features of his job to his attention and teaches him the proper responses. Good training produces not only new knowledge, but new skills, wants (motives), response sets, habits and attitudes.

Attention comes from attention attractors.

Attention goes to whichever attention attractors have the greatest power at the time.

We naturally notice certain types of occurrence over others. For instance, anything threatening or potentially dangerous has great power over our attention. Examples would include something large which is moving rapidly toward us, something unusually loud or bright, or something drastically different from normal. Our reactions to these things are inborn and automatic.

In other cases, we have learned to notice occurrences or states of affairs because they indicate a matter of importance to us. Psychologists have identified two mechanisms by which we develop these response patterns: "Classical Conditioning" and "Operant Conditioning." Classical conditioning occurs when a stimulus is closely associated with the occurrence of an automatic (involuntary) response. Operant conditioning obeys the Law of Effect, mentioned earlier.

Habits and *sets* are other learned-response mechanisms. Habits are formed by repetition. We may be so used to seeing certain things or people that we do not really look at them. We respond by habit to a few stimuli. Thus, we may fail to notice that our house is cluttered if it is always cluttered. Unfortunately for us, someone new, or a better housekeeper, will be sure to notice.

Sets are psychological reaction potentials which we can create intentionally. For instance, a person driving through fog will "set" himself to carefully watch the road ahead and react quickly to anything he sees. A building guard may "set" himself to hear unusual noises. The mother of a young child will "set" herself to wake if her child cries in the night.

"Automatic" actions and reactions come from habit.

Habit can short-cut the causal chain of events that first leads to an action or reaction.

When you first learned to drive, you thought carefully about how to act and react in every traffic situation. Later, when your driving had become habitual, you reacted "automatically" to changing conditions. You skipped many of the intermediate steps of attending, identifying, thinking, rethinking, deciding and feeling that were once essential parts of your driving.

The same kind of short-cutting can occur for any step from attention and thought to decision-making, feeling and action.

Habits *can* be of great benefit. If we develop useful habits in ourselves and others, much time and effort can be saved by not having to rethink each step of a recurring task. We can react quickly and correctly through an habitual response pattern.

When a new reaction is needed, however, habit can be a major obstacle. In these instances, we need to resist our habitual tendencies, select a new behavior, and strengthen it until it becomes the dominant response.

SUMMARY

Human action is brought about through a chain of causes and effects. The same is true of human reactions and experiences. The causal connections can be summarized as follows:

- Action is caused by Feeling,
- Feeling is caused by Belief,
- Belief is caused by Thinking,
- Thinking is caused by Wants and Experience,
- Wants are caused by Experience (and Inborn Mechanisms),
- Experience is caused by Attention,
- Attention is caused by Attention Attractors,
- Attention Attractors are caused by Inborn Predispositions and Earlier Experience,
- Habit can short-cut any of the steps in the causal chain.

(See the diagram at the end of this chapter for an illustration of these connections.)

APPLICATIONS

The practical importance of these causal connections lies in the use of appropriate causes to bring about desired results.

If you want action of a certain kind, the causal connection of action with feeling tells you that you can obtain the action if you can create the right kind of feeling. For instance, by creating strong emotions such as anger, enthusiasm, determination or pride, you might cause an employee to try harder.

If you want a certain feeling, the causal connection of feelings with beliefs tells you to create beliefs that will cause the desired emotion. Employees will feel enthusiasm if they believe, "We are going to achieve something great." They will feel confidence if they believe your plan will work and they can do their parts with credit.

Similar applications can be made for each of the above causal laws. In the topics to follow, you will find that all the methods described are based on causal connections such as these.

EXAMPLES

For each of the following, try to formulate your own answer before reading the discussion.

1. A manager criticizes an employee for doing a poor job on an assignment. What effect will this criticism have on the employee's motivation to do a good job in the future? **What is your answer?**

*Discussion:*This case illustrates the importance of internal reactions in determining the nature of an experience. If the employee is generally good, the criticism will have a powerful motivational effect; he will try hard to do a good job next time. If the employee is generally poor, however, the criticism will have little effect in motivating future improvement.

The reason for this is the level of adaptation in each case. A good employee is used to being praised, not criticized. The criticism he receives is more painful because he is not accustomed to it. He also has an established image of himself as one who does good work. The criticism challenges this self-image and provides an additional motive for him to improve.

On the other hand, the poor employee is used to being criticized. This one instance is no different from any other, so it has little effect. Because he does not regard himself as someone who does good work, there is no positive self-image to protect.

2. What experiences would cause a customer to want to continue buying your product instead of a competitor's? **What is your answer?**

Discussion: First, she may be well satisfied with the performance of your product. If it costs less, this could be a major incentive. The extra service you provide may be the deciding factor. In any case, the direct experience of the customer is the most powerful determinant of her future wants.

Second, she may have tried the competitor's product and had an unpleasant experience with it. You can gain a business advantage whenever your competitors make mistakes or do not care enough to deliver a satisfying experience to customers.

3. What wants or motives could cause a person to do superior work, more than just what is required? **What is your answer?**

Discussion: Good work can be motivated by many wants. Some people work well because they are ambitious and want to get ahead; others, because of pride in their performance. In times of economic hardship when jobs are scarce, people may work harder just to keep the jobs they have. Some simply enjoy doing good work.

4. What kind of thinking would produce a belief among staff members that the boss does not care about the welfare of his employees?
What is your answer?

Discussion: People will think about matters related to their wants and based upon their experience. Therefore, the boss's speech and actions will be evaluated most carefully when they affect employees' interests.

Does this boss take time to show a personal interest in individual employees, or does he only talk to them when he wants them to do something for him? Does he ever sacrifice his own interests to help others, or is he "strictly business" and "by the book"? Does he give credit to others when it is due, or keep it all for himself?

These behaviors may not seem important to a "Boss" type of manager, but they stand out in employees' experience and are directly related to their wants. Naturally, they will think about them and could easily arrive at the negative opinions expressed.

5. What beliefs would produce a feeling of self-confidence?
What is your answer?

Discussion: People feel self-confidence if, and only if, they believe, "I can do this; I can handle it; I will succeed."

6. What feeling, emotion or inner-urge would cause a customer to purchase a major product such as an automobile?
What is your answer?

Discussion: The ultimate emotional state might be quite complicated. It could be a combination of the very practical decision that this is the best car to suit her needs, the very egotistical feeling that it will impress her friends, and the momentary impulse to make any decision which will settle the matter.

Emotions used to close automobile sales include
- desire for the car,
- pride,
- a favorable self-image,
- social acceptance,
- getting a good deal (self-satisfaction, winning),
- approval of the sales people,
- confidence in the sales people and the dealership,
- urgency because the opportunity might be lost,
- attraction of the "sweeteners" (additional benefits offered near the end of the sale to clinch the agreement).

DIAGRAM: CAUSES AND EFFECTS
LEADING TO ACTION

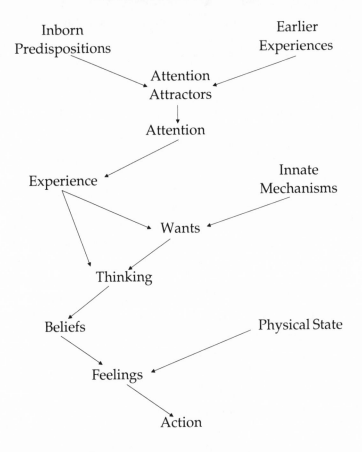

Modifiers:
1. Wants, thinking, beliefs, feelings and actions immediately become part of experience and can influence future wants, thinking, beliefs, feelings and actions.
2. Habit can short-cut any of the steps in the causal chain.

CHAPTER 5

THINKING MORE PRODUCTIVELY AND GETTING OTHERS TO THINK

The Importance of Good Thinking for Managers

An essential part of your job as a manager is to think for the group. You must plan, make decisions, solve problems, create new projects and methods, discover the truth, notice what is happening, recognize its significance, and anticipate future developments and needs.

You are also supposed to obtain adequate work from other people. Since good performance from employees requires them to think productively, you should know how to lead others to think. Ideally, you will manage your department so that creative and productive thinking are encouraged. Employees who are trained to think productively can evaluate their own work, exercise good judgement, and learn to manage themselves.

The Causes of Poor Thinking

When we think poorly, it is because of the way thinking is caused. Thinking is very highly influenced by wants, that is, it is purposeful. This makes us prone to make mistakes because we think toward a conclusion we *want* rather than ones that are true.

When this happens, we engage in

- *Wishful Thinking:* we want something so badly that we ignore the evidence and decide that what we want is going to happen anyway;
- *Prejudiced Thinking:* we have already decided on an issue and guide our thinking to that conclusion only, ignoring any contrary evidence;
- *Rationalizing:* we justify what we have done by selective consideration of evidence, again ignoring any contrary evidence;
- *Being Closed-minded:* we do not even want to think about an issue, for fear we may find out that we are wrong;
- *Jumping to Conclusions:* we are in too much of a hurry for an answer and are unwilling to think long or carefully enough to arrive at the truth.

Other causes of poor thinking include the following:
1. We make mistakes when we do not have adequate information on the subject of our thought. This problem can be overcome, to some extent, when we learn to think

first about what information we need in order to solve the problem at hand. Obviously, misinformation (false beliefs) will lead to false conclusions. We must be as sure as we can be of our information.

2. Habit in thought can keep us from discovering a solution for our problems. We tend to see only one side of an issue. Our thinking becomes fixed on one aspect or one unworkable plan. We fail to see and consider alternatives.

3. We make mistakes when strong feelings cloud our thinking. If such emotions are aroused, we may think about those feelings to the exclusion of everything else. Good thinking requires a "cool head," so that alternatives can be considered and facts recognized for what they are.

4. People think poorly when they do not take the time and trouble to think well. Good thinking is almost always careful and precise. Some find this tedious and difficult, so they take short cuts which lead to false conclusions.

5. Most people have received little or no instruction in how to think. They do not realize that their thinking is faulty or that they could do much better. Furthermore, there are factors in our society which actively discourage good thinking. Advertisers, politicians and others seeking to influence public opinion often use fallacious logic when they have no sound arguments to support their positions. People in authority may discourage thinking because they do not want others to think independently but only to obey orders.

Mistakes in reasoning are called "fallacies." Some common fallacies are these:

- *Begging the Question*: when the conclusion is already assumed in the evidence given;
- *Irrelevant Conclusion*: when the evidence given may support a related conclusion, but not the one drawn;

- *Hasty Generalization*: when a general rule is inferred from too few or inappropriate cases;
- *Appeal to Force*: when someone tries to prove his point by threatening or frightening his opponents;
- *Appeal to Authority*: when someone tries to prove his point by citing some authority who agrees with it.

These last two are common among Bosses. They justify their opinions by saying, "I am right because I am the Boss." This may be relevant in deciding what will be done, but it does not make it correct. What makes something right (acceptable as true) is the evidence and logical reasoning that supports it.

Texts and courses in logic are good sources of information on common fallacies and how to avoid them. You may want to read some of the psychological research reports on thinking, as well.

Not all poor thinking is fallacious. Some is just fruitless. Fruitless thinking never reaches a useful conclusion. Here are some typical examples:

- *Wishful thinking*, which is out of line with what will actually happen;
- *Worrying*, which goes around in a circle, never arriving at a conclusion or a decision to act;
- *Blaming*, where we try to decide who is to blame instead of trying to find a solution to the problem;
- *Regret*, where we go over and over a past event that we can no longer change;
- *Thinking about any problem* we are not going to do anything to solve, for example, those global concerns that are far beyond our powers to influence.

How To Think More Productively

The first step in improving any skill is deciding to do

it. That means saying to yourself, "I will accomplish this!" This is not the same as deciding, "I will try this." When we decide to try something, we have only promised ourselves to *try*. We could satisfy our promise by just going through the motions. When we decide to *do* something, we have promised ourselves to succeed. Therefore, we cannot quit until it is accomplished. (Just as deciding to become an effective leader and manager implies a commitment to mastering the necessary skills.)

Productive thinking has these three stages:
1. **Asking questions;**
2. **Searching for answers;**
3. **Evaluating the answers.**

The three steps lead to a conclusion or decision. At that point, thinking on the topic stops. Action or different thinking follows.

The first stage of thinking is asking a question. This states the problem to be solved. It is usually a fact or belief we need to know to accomplish some goal.

The search for an answer begins with a mental search through the knowledge and experience stored in our memory. We use the thinking skills we have learned, putting information together until we reach a possible answer.

Sometimes we have sufficient information in memory. If not, we search for ideas in other ways: in books or magazines, by asking other people, by observations, by trial and error, or even through complex research projects. When we cannot find an immediate answer, we shift our thinking to a related question, such as, "How can I find a satisfactory answer?" or "What do I need to know first?" or "How shall I start?"

Once we have some possible answers, we evaluate them by submission to various tests. We may ask, "Would this method work in this particular situation?"; "Would I be able to do this?"; "Have I made any mistakes in reasoning in reaching this conclusion?"; "Am I sure of the facts used in this reasoning?"

Another way we evaluate answers is by comparing them with our other knowledge and by drawing inferences from them to see if they are reasonable. Sometimes we will conduct extensive experiments or research projects to evaluate an answer. Other times, the evaluation process is so fast it appears to be automatic.

Consider the following line of thought. Although this example is a simple one, it reveals the basic structure of thinking used in the most complex reasoning.

> Question: "How can I improve the speed of order processing in the office?"
>
> Initial Answer: "I do not know."
>
> Related Questions: "How can I find out? What are some possible ways? What has worked at other places?"
>
> Search for Answers: "I could...read industry magazines, take a course at the university, call in a consultant, talk to Joe at XYZ Corporation..."
>
> Evaluating and Selecting an Answer: "Here is a method that worked at XYZ Corporation. I will try it here."

To increase the productivity of your thinking, start by asking yourself questions. Look for problems to solve. Do not let yourself be satisfied with things as they are. Ask, "How can we improve?" Then, find and try out different answers.

Planning (*"practical reasoning"*) is different from factual reasoning. In reasoning about matters of fact, the conclusion reached is a statement of fact or belief. In planning and practical reasoning, the conclusion is a decision of what to do.

Practical reasoning assumes that something is wanted. Reasoning is done to discover how to achieve it. Therefore, *the first step in practical reasoning is to decide on the purpose or goal to be achieved.* The more precisely this can be stated, the better the subsequent thinking is likely to be.

The next step is to ask how the goal can be reached and then to search for answers. These become possible decisions, plans and strategies.

Next, evaluate the possible plans and strategies relative to their total advantages and disadvantages. Judge them according to the probability that they will succeed, their side-effects (results in addition to that desired) and their costs (including money, time, effort, reputation, worry, etc.).

From the plans evaluated, choose one as "the best." (Keep in mind that one alternative is to do nothing; another is to decide that the issue cannot be decided.) Then, make a decision to act according to the chosen plan.

Thinking stops and action begins whenever a satisfactory decision has been made. Before doing this, however, you should formulate some contingency plans. These will be implemented in case the chosen plan fails or it proves to be too difficult or expensive.

Creative thinking differs from both factual and practical reasoning. In each of the latter, we are extracting conclusions from information we already have. In creative thought, we generate ideas which go beyond our present knowledge.

Reasoning By Analogy is a powerful method you can use for generating new ideas. An analogy is any similarity between the subject and something else. For example, there is a structural similarity between the human nervous system and electrical circuits. If you are doing research on the operation of the nervous system, you might look at the operation of electric circuits for ideas.

To apply Reasoning By Analogy, ask, "Does this remind me of anything?" What you think about need not be relevant to the subject in any way except that it somehow reminds you of it. (In order to discover new ideas, you need to look in areas not normally considered relevant.)

Groups can reason by analogy through "Brainstorming." The first rule of brainstorming is that any ideas are allowed, no matter how "crazy." No one may criticize anyone's suggestions. *After* brainstorming is completed, the group can evaluate the resulting ideas for possible use.

How To Generate Productive Thinking In Others

The three stages of productive thought can be used as steps for guiding the thoughts of others. *To cause a person to think, ask questions.* These questions should be carefully phrased to be relevant to the topic and point the way toward the desired conclusions.

Once you have started a person's thinking through the use of questions, you allow her to take the next steps herself, namely, searching for answers and evaluating them. You cannot provide the answers or you will be doing the thinking.

You must also allow the person to evaluate her own answers, for the same reasons.

If, at some point, the person runs into trouble with her thinking, you should not "help" by providing answers or evaluations. Instead, ask additional questions, ones which will guide her to overcoming the difficulty for herself.

By proceeding in this way, you avoid arousing the other person's resistance, you keep two sides from being formed, and you allow her to reach her own conclusions.

Besides questions, you may use suggestions, pose a problem, quote another person's opinion, or present a dilemma. You could also express surprise or other emotions which would encourage the person to take an interest in the topic.

Productive and creative thinking in a group can be encouraged in the same way that any desired behavior is encouraged. You urge people to think; you praise and reward them when they do.

This also implies that you do not punish them for thinking. Do not criticize or ridicule their ideas when these are not as good as you hoped they would be. Do not tell them what you think or try to make them accept your opinion. Let people think of their own answers. Be tolerant of differing opinions, backgrounds, and points of view. These are the source of new ideas.

The two major limitations on thinking are experience and wants. You cannot get a person to think about matters which are totally beyond his experience. Train and retrain new employees, then allow time for on-the-job learning before expecting them to think independently.

People are caused to think most about things connected with their wants. Therefore, be sure to tell employees and others how they will benefit by thinking about the matters you wish to discuss with them. Do not assume that people will have maximum team spirit or an overwhelming desire to cooperate at every moment. For these to exist, they also must be connected with personal wants.

Why is leading others to think so important?

As true leaders, we do not try to force or deceive people. We help them see for themselves that what we propose is also the best thing for them.

By allowing people to think for themselves, we avoid arousing their resistance or resentment toward someone telling them what to do or believe. We also help them develop their abilities for responsible self-management and for solving problems themselves. Finally, permitting different viewpoints provides a rich source of new ideas and methods, which we can use to further our goals and the goals of the group.

SUMMARY

Thinking productively is crucial for a Leader/ Manager because an important part of his job is to think, plan and solve problems for the group. The leader must also lead others to think in order to gain their willing cooperation and thus, maximize performance.

The basic structure of productive thought is (1) asking questions, (2) searching for answers, and (3) evaluating the answers and selecting the best. We lead others to think by asking them questions, allowing them to search for answers, and helping them to evaluate their answers.

There are several effective methods for improving thinking skills in individuals and groups.

APPLICATIONS

Learn to recognize and avoid fruitless and fallacious thinking patterns. For instance, do you know how to break out of the fruitless pattern of worrying?

First, you could recognize that worry is motivated by strong wants and a fear of loss. Try to control or offset this source. Next, recognize that worrying is thinking in a circle. Break out of the circle by asking a new question which will lead to an answer. The question might be, "Is there anything I can do now that might improve the situation?" or "How can I direct my thoughts that will lead to some useful conclusion or decision and will drive this fruitless worrying from my mind?"

Another example is guilt. How would you overcome this painful emotion?

Guilt is the feeling which follows when you believe you have done something wrong to another person. It is hard to escape because you cannot change what is past. To eliminate it, find some action you can take to make up for your misdeeds. Ask yourself, "What can I do now that will adequately atone for the injury I have caused?" When you find a suitable answer, put it into effect. Then, instead of just saying, "I did wrong," you can tell yourself, "I did wrong but I made up for it."

The following cases illustrate the application of productive thinking techniques in management. Try to analyze these situations and solve the problems presented before reading the discussion.

EXAMPLES

1. "I am a shop supervisor. My assistant, who I hope will take over my job someday, does not think enough before suggesting something. He comes up with a lot of ideas, most of which are unworkable. I have to waste my time listening to these wild schemes and telling him why they will not work. I would not dare let him make any actual decisions! How can I get my assistant to think things through all the way and consider the consequences of his ideas?"

What is your answer?

Discussion: There are several problems here. First, the supervisor's attitude toward him cannot be very encouraging to the assistant. He is punished for the thinking he does by the criticism he always receives. Second, the assistant has little reason to think carefully or evaluate his ideas before suggesting them. He knows that the supervisor will do the evaluating for him. If anyone is to seriously consider the consequences of his ideas, he must believe that they might be implemented. To give him a reason for thinking better, he should be made responsible for the results of his suggestions in actual practice. He also needs practice in applications in order to learn what works and what does not.

A good learning program would result if the supervisor gave the assistant some decisions to make on matters where mistakes would not be too costly. As the assistant learned from these, he could be given responsibility in more important areas.

2. "I am credit manager for a large department store. Part of my job is handling people who are extremely upset about denial of credit or further credit, as for a major purchase. When these people get to me, they are usually furious. How should I handle these irate customers? How can I get them to calm down and think rationally about their credit problems? How can I get them to quit blaming the store and start taking responsibility themselves for their credit standing?"
What is your answer?

Discussion: This is an ideal situation for leading people to think. To begin, remember to never argue with people when they are angry. Allow them to have their say. Listen attentively. Show them that you are not setting yourself up against them.

When they have finished "telling you off," they will calm down. Then ask them, "Would you like me to go over this with you and see if we can find a solution?" Phrased in this way, the question should bring a positive response. Next, ask them questions of fact about their wants and their present credit situation. Explain very briefly what you are allowed to do by store policy in cases like this. Immediately return to questions which direct their thinking to what *they* can do to improve their credit. For example, you might ask, "Could you pay your present account down to $200 or less?" or "Do you have anyone who might co-sign your loan for you?" Offer to do whatever you can to help, provided they will take the steps you need.

When they begin to think in terms of what they can do to improve their credit standing, then they are beginning to assume responsibility. This is the only way they will overcome these problems, of course.

If you are able to handle this case successfully, you will be exercising leadership. The store will benefit by retaining these customers and all those who might have been lost if they had complained to their friends and relatives. The customers will benefit by working out their credit problems. You will gain by doing your job well, avoiding additional conflict and being of valuable service to everyone involved.

3. "When new employees come through my department, it is part of my responsibility to train them. After awhile, they are supposed to know what to do and quit relying on me to tell them. The problem is, some never reach this stage. They keep coming to me for answers they should figure out for themselves. How can I help these people without doing the work for them? How can I get them to think for themselves?"
What is your answer?

Discussion: When employees are new, they cannot think effectively because they do not have the necessary experience. They recognize this and will willingly follow your directions.

The normal next step is taken when they recognize that they have enough knowledge and can do the work on their own. Those who do not reach this stage may be unsure of their abilities, trying to avoid responsibility or just wanting you to do this part of their work for them.

When the time comes for a person to start making his own decisions, you must stop making them for him. Do not give answers to questions or tell the person what to do. Insist that he think these out for himself. If you do help, ask questions that will direct his thinking in the right direction. Ask other questions that will help him see a way around problems. For example, you could ask, "What have you done so far?" "What would be a logical next step?" or "What are some possible solutions to the problem?"

Sometimes, you can direct thinking by rephrasing a statement as a question. You could ask, "Would doing ABC work in this case?" Other times, you will ask open-ended questions, where there is no hint of the answer in the question itself. An example would be, "What will you do next?" The skillful use of each type will come with practice.

You can employ a similar technique to help your children with their homework or other tasks where they should be learning to work for themselves. This requires some patience and practice on your part, but the results are worth the effort.

CHAPTER 6

AVOIDING RESISTANCE
AND RESENTMENT

The Costs of Resistance

When employees resist management, either actively or passively, the cost of operations doubles. The first cost is that of overcoming the resistance. The second cost is that of lost opportunities, the production that might have been achieved with the time and effort that went into resisting.

Managers must avoid arousing resistance whenever possible. This is most difficult if they do not realize that their own behavior is the cause. We may be creating our own problems without knowing it. It will be difficult, as well, if features of organizational structure or operations are causing the resistance. As managers, we must contend with the results even when the causes are beyond our control.

The costs of resistance are dramatically illustrated when organizations solve long-standing resistance problems. Many have achieved increases of several hundred percent in productivity and profitability. Conflict can ruin a company; harmony and cooperation can make it.

Causes of Resistance and Resentment

Resistance is the feeling we get when we think we are being forced to do something or put up with something we do not want. It is also the act of resisting which follows from this feeling.

Some of the things we do not want and which cause resistance are

- other people making us do anything, or trying to do so;
- being dominated by others;
- being criticized or blamed;
- being embarrassed or made to lose face;
- being treated unfairly;
- losing in a contest, competition, debate or fight;
- being tricked, deceived or manipulated;
- having others plot or work against us.

Resentment is the feeling we have toward anyone or any group that prevents us from having what we want, or tries to do so. Resentment is strongest when we believe that our antagonist had no right to interfere with us as he did. We feel resentful whenever we form the belief, "He had no right to treat me that way," or "He should not have done that to me." Resentment is lingering anger. It is the motivation behind revenge.

We cause resistance in people anytime they have the impression that we are pressuring them, whether we intended to do so or not. Pressure exists if people think it does.

All of us are more likely to feel pressured at certain times. Fatigue and illness make us especially sensitive, as do personal dislikes, distrust and general unhappiness. In these cases, even a trivial incident can set off a major reaction.

Anyone dissatisfied with his job, his marriage, his life or himself will generalize this feeling to other areas. Some people make a habit of resisting any attempt to get them to do something. Others make a habit of resenting everything. When dealing with these types of people, you should use additional care.

You will cause others to resist and resent you if your actions reflect an attitude of superiority, dominance, over-confidence, selfishness, unfriendliness, dislike of others, or resentment of others. People judge you by your motives. If they think you are trying to get the better of them, they will resist.

How to Avoid Resistance and Resentment From Others

Attitudes and Actions to Avoid:
- Attitudes of superiority.
- Use of force, pressure or formal authority.
- Tactics of deception and manipulation.
- Making the other person lose face in any way.
- Letting two sides be created. (Do not let him think you are against him.)
- Arguing.
- Use of criticism.
- Rushing or hurrying a person. (Control your impatience.)

- Confusing others. (Speak in language they understand.)
- Losing control of your emotions. (Avoid impatience, unfriendliness, irritation, anger, resentment and personal dislike.)
- Assuming that you cannot possibly be wrong. (Keep an open mind. This encourages him to do likewise.)
- Blaming him if you arouse his resistance or resentment. (Do not blame yourself either.)

What to do instead:

However much we wish to avoid it, managers and others in positions of authority or responsibility must sometimes act in ways that cause resistance. We must get our jobs done, which means obtaining adequate performance from others, even if they do not like what we are doing or do not want to cooperate.

Avoid causing resistance to whatever extent you can. Then, do the following to offset any resistance and resentment that you cannot avoid.

First, check your own motives. Make sure you are not after a one-sided advantage and that you truly want to help the people who work with you.

Second, when dealing with "touchy" issues, keep it light. Do not make the occasion overly serious, but use good humor, good fellowship, friendliness, and good will. Keep people from dwelling too much on the unpleasant aspects of a situation.

Third, and most importantly, show a personal interest and concern for the other people. People often resent the way something is done more than the action itself. They may see the necessity for what you ask, but they do not like you making them do it. Counteract this response by demonstrating your sincere concern for their wants and desires, show sympathy for their feelings, make them know that you want to help them, and express appreciation for the cooperation they have given. Treat others as friends and equals. Show your confidence in them, that they will do the right thing.

Fourth, always give people some choice. If you are going to require an action, allow them to choose some feature of the activity, such as how or when they will do it. Thus, instead of saying, "Put on the collars, then finish the painting," you could give a choice: "Would you rather put the collars on now or do the painting first?" Allow your employees freedom to choose as many matters as you can. This permits people to fulfill the psychological need to exercise some control over their situations. Having a feeling of control greatly reduces the amount of pressure they feel; by reducing overall pressure, you increase their ability to endure it during those times when you must insist on extra performance. You also demonstrate that you are concerned for them and are trying to help.

Fifth, clear the air when resistance and resentment are aroused. Do not blame or criticize anyone, but do allow an opportunity for all to express their feelings about the subject. Expressing ill feelings helps us to get rid of them. Repressed resentment can feed on itself, growing stronger until it erupts in anger and conflict.

Sixth, use methods of leadership in working with all people: lead them to think instead of telling them, create cooperation instead of conflict, use persuasion instead of force or manipulation. Your employees *want* you to fulfill the functions of leadership. They will not resist or resent what they want.

SUMMARY

Resistance is an automatic reaction to perceived pressure. To avoid arousing it, avoid doing those things that people do not want. These include the use of force, authority, criticism and manipulation. Offset any unavoidable resistance or resentment by demonstrating your personal concern for others and your genuine desire to help them. Whenever possible, give them a choice.

APPLICATIONS

Here are two exercises that should help you reduce resistance and resentment in your organization.

1. Analyze your organization for structural and procedural features that cause resistance or resentment among those who work there. Is the chief executive a "Boss"? Is there a tradition of authoritarian management? Is the organization impersonal and bureaucratic? Is there a militant union or a history of labor conflict? Is the work itself unpleasant or demeaning? Are the physical surroundings unpleasant?

When you have a list of negative factors, exercise your leadership skills by finding ways to remove or reduce them. Plan ways to offset the negative features with positive ones. At the very least, show that you are aware of the problems and want to improve the situation if you can.

2. Find out what behaviors of yours are causing people to resist or resent you, then find ways to change these. Substitute more attractive methods. Practice showing people your personal concern for them. Institute leadership training programs for all managers and supervisors,

to decrease any resistance caused by overly authoritarian methods or inconsiderate treatment.

EXAMPLES

1. Resistance to Change

Suppose you must introduce major changes in your department. Some employees will benefit from these changes; others may not. Everyone will have to learn new job skills; virtually all procedures will be different. How could you reduce the resistance to change that employees are sure to feel?

What is your answer?

Discussion: An analysis of the situation would show which aspects of the new procedures people dislike the most. You may be able to modify procedures to remove some of these features. Still, any change requires employees to do some additional work. They will have to learn new skills and adjust to new methods. They will want to maintain their present positions and will probably worry about the ultimate outcome.

Negatives can be removed or reduced, however, if you provide some or all of the following:

- incentives (rewards) for making the changes;
- forewarning and explanation of the changes;
- effective training in the new job skills;
- a trial period or a transition period;
- an opportunity for employees to influence the new work requirements through consulting with management before final decisions are made;
- an opportunity to influence their work through

group decision making on whatever issues can be left to employee discretion (always give people some choices to make themselves);

- symbolic values for success, such as presenting the changes as an exciting challenge, recognizing achievement and tying group and individual rewards to group success.

2. Resentment of a New Supervisor

Suppose you are selected to be the new supervisor of a department where the old supervisor was very popular. Suppose you are younger than many of the workers there and have specialized training which they do not understand. Suppose you have no direct experience with the people or the particular operation you will be supervising. In these circumstances, you are extremely likely to encounter resentment and resistance. What will you do to overcome it?

What is your answer?

Discussion: Many of the techniques for reducing resistance to change will be applicable here. In addition to using these, you could

- adjust the rate at which you introduce changes in the department so that additional resistance is not aroused (do not go too fast or too slow);
- be sure to have the support of upper management; this should be made clear through a meeting or ceremony in which you are officially introduced as the supervisor; the positions of others in the group should be made clear as well;

- consult with employees; this will show your respect and concern for them; also, it will help you learn about the people and the operation;
- make personal, one-to-one contacts with employees; ask for their help and support; find some who will be your supporters or future lieutenants;
- be patient; expect it to take time; continue to practice good leadership; win their confidence in your right to hold this position through your outstanding performance.

CHAPTER 7

STAYING OUT OF
USELESS ARGUMENTS

Good Arguments and Bad Arguments

In the study of logic and the practice of law, to "argue"
is to support a belief by presenting evidence (facts) and
sound reasoning which leads to that conclusion. Obviously, there is nothing wrong with this. In fact, this kind
of argument can be an excellent aid to decision making
and group thinking.

In everyday usage, however, to "argue" means to
have a verbal battle. Each person tries to force his opponent to concede. This type of argument is more a
heated assertion of opinion than a purposeful discussion.
It rarely results in agreement but usually results in each
person more entrenched in his position than before. It is
this kind of argument which we wish to avoid.

The problems with arguing include these:

1. Arguing is an ineffective method for reaching agreement. It is a waste of time and effort.

2. Arguing is detrimental to any future efforts to gain agreement. Argument starts when someone resists what you are saying. Arguing does not reduce this resistance, however; it makes it worse. Continuing the argument arouses ill will, resentment, distrust, anger and entrenchment of opinion. These, in turn, interfere with clear thinking, making it unlikely that the matter will ever be resolved reasonably.

Too much argument can lead to habitual arguing, which results in nothing being done. Some people use argument as a method for getting out of work.

Causes of Argument

Arguments of the verbal-battle kind are likely to occur whenever we make positive statements of our opinions to someone who is not immediately prepared to agree. People will tend to argue when the matter is important to them or when it arouses their strong emotions. They are most likely to defend their beliefs if

-   they identify themselves closely with their opinions;
-   their opinions are connected with their strongest wants;
-   they feel they would lose face by not defending their beliefs;
-   they consider themselves experts on the subject, or at least have a greater right to express an opinion than the speaker;
-   they are generally unable to tolerate any viewpoint but their own.

A person may resist you if she has negative feelings toward you. She may dislike you, distrust you or feel superior to you. She may be resentful toward you because you give the impression of being opinionated, intolerant or arrogant.

Some people argue because they want to argue. This can occur if the person

- enjoys arguing;
- is in the habit of arguing;
- likes to make trouble;
- is trying to make you angry or gain some other advantage.

How To Avoid Useless Argument

1. Make sure of your purposes. Are you trying to make the other person admit that you are right and he is wrong? Do you think of him as an opponent? If so, he will quickly sense what is happening and will defend himself by arguing.

2. Avoid conditions that promote conflict; seek conditions which promote harmony.

For example, do not try to convince someone who has disagreed with you in front of others. He cannot change his position without losing face. Discuss the matter with him privately, at another time, when neither of you has to play to an audience.

Do not try to discuss a matter with someone who is not in the least interested in the topic at that time.

Do not criticize a person or her opinions. Do not act as if you know everything or could not possibly be wrong. Do not interrupt her or give the impression you think her stupid or misinformed. Be patient. Do not become upset if she does not agree with you. Do not blame her if you cannot obtain her immediate agreement. (Do not blame yourself either.)

Instead of these, try to establish an agreeable relationship. Pay attention to what she has to say. Allow her time to express herself. Keep the discussion calm and unemotional, so that good thinking can occur. Be friendly. Preserve your own good humor.

3. Do not state your opinions as if they were absolute facts. Naturally, you think your ideas are correct. Otherwise, you would not hold them. But it is essential to remember: You can always be wrong, in some way, on any issue. You probably believe that other people are mistaken in many of their beliefs, beliefs which they hold just as strongly as you do yours. Therefore, label your opinions for what they are. Say, "The way it looks to me is ..." or "I feel this way about it ..."

Likewise, do not challenge another's opinions by blunt assertion of your disagreement. Instead, use questions to get him to explain or rethink his position.

4. If challenged, you need not always defend yourself. A vigorous defense gives the impression of insecurity on your part. People wonder, "If he is so sure he is right, why is he arguing so hard?" A strong defense can also antagonize people and encourage them to defend their opinions in return. The result is more argument.

5. Once an argument is started, you can stop it. Quit trying to prove that you are right and he or she is wrong. Do not attack. Do not defend yourself if attacked. No one can make you argue if you know how to avoid it.

6. Convert an argument into a discussion. Concentrate on what is right instead of who is right. Ask the other person questions. Ignore points of disagreement, but say when you agree with him. Introduce ideas for discussion

without asserting them. Try to get him to stop arguing and start thinking.

SUMMARY

Verbal battle is an ineffective way of convincing people. Avoid it by avoiding the conditions which cause it, including personal dislikes, threatening topics and public debates. State your opinions as opinions, not as absolute facts. Ask people questions to show your interest in them and to get them to think instead of argue. Concentrate on what is right rather than who is right.

APPLICATIONS

Some people have more trouble with argument than others. If you are one who does, analyze your feelings and behavior. Do you feel insecure? Do you use argument to defend yourself? Do you argue to gain an advantage over others or to establish your superiority over them? Are you opinionated (holding beliefs more strongly than is reasonable)? Do you have habits of expressing yourself that irritate people or cause others to resist you? Do you have trouble controlling your temper?

Decide that you really want to change your behavior, then use the methods discussed. Find substitute actions to replace those that lead to conflict.

Use the same principles to reduce arguing between other people. Get them to think by using questions and suggestions. Convert the argument into a discussion. If appropriate, point out the futility of arguing and explain the advantages of avoiding it. Then, show them the methods to accomplish this.

EXAMPLES

1. "I know a union representative who feels it is his job to always argue against management. This is especially true during negotiations, when he tries to gain advantages for labor through strong assertions of his beliefs and demands. Is this a situation where arguing is really the best way?"
What is your answer?

Discussion: It is true that a representative of a conflicting group is expected to stand up for the interests of that group. A union representative should forcefully express the views of the membership and strive to achieve as many of their goals as possible. Argument is a forceful way to bring issues to everyone's attention.

It is also true that agreement with management must eventually be reached. For this to happen, verbal battle must be suspended and discussion started toward those goals that are common to labor and management. The union representative must know when to stop arguing and start sincere discussion toward solving the problems and reaching a settlement.

2. "A friend of mine cannot discuss a matter without becoming emotionally involved and turning the discussion into a heated argument. Can anything be done to change him?"
What is your answer?

Discussion: You may not be able to do anything except to avoid such discussions when your friend is present. He would have to realize that he has a problem and also want to change. Even then, it could be difficult.

If this were a subordinate instead of a friend, you could point out his behavior pattern to him. Explain why it is a problem for the company. You would be within your rights to ask him to stop doing it.

A later chapter on correcting faults covers several approaches to this kind of problem.

3. "The night-shift workers at the power plant argue constantly. They like to bait one or two of the workers until they get them involved too. They will defend absurd ideas just to get an argument going. Is this a problem?"

What is your answer?

Discussion: The type of argument described is not a genuine disagreement. It is a way to pass the time. It is a form of entertainment, a game. As long as no one is offended or upset, and it does not interfere with the work, it can be regarded as a harmless amusement.

CHAPTER 8

WINNING
PEOPLE'S CONFIDENCE

When people have confidence in you, everything else becomes easy. They will believe what you say, do what you ask, cooperate, learn, work willingly and even like you. Lack of confidence causes all the opposite reactions. If they do not trust you, people may resist everything you say and may not cooperate with you on anything.

There are two major obstacles to obtaining people's confidence. The first is that confidence does not exist unless it is created. Many people expect others to have confidence in them. However, people's natural first response is caution and a withholding of trust. We tend to distrust all strangers and most other people until they have proved to us that they are worthy of our confidence.

The second obstacle is that confidence is difficult to win but easy to lose. We may work with someone for years before winning his trust. But after only one negative experience, he may never trust us again. Thus, consistency is a primary requirement for creating and maintaining confidence.

The Nature of Confidence

Confidence is a feeling. It is the feeling we have when we believe something strongly. Thus, if we believe that someone will do as he promised, we have confidence in that person to keep his promises.

We form our beliefs about people by our direct experience with them. Lacking direct experience, we go by their reputation or the reputation of their profession or group. We also judge people by comparison with ourselves, with what we wish they were, or with our previous opinions of them.

Full confidence in a person requires two types of confidence. First is confidence in his *motives*. We are most concerned with those motives which affect us, that is, with what we want from this person. Therefore, we wish to know if he is motivated to help us as well as himself, if he generally wants to keep his promises, if he plays by the rules, if he is willing to go out of his way to help others, if he likes to work or is lazy, and similar matters.

If we believe in an individual's motives, then we say to ourselves, "He wants to do the right things where I am concerned," and "I can count on him to try to do what is expected." The resulting feeling is called "trust." The more certain we are of a person's honorable motives, the stronger is our feeling of trust in him.

The second type of confidence is confidence in *abilities*. Again, we are most concerned with those abilities which would be useful for our interests. When we believe the individual has these abilities, we say, "He can do what is required," or "He has the ability to handle this task." Consequently, we feel confidence in or respect for his ability.

We must win both their trust and respect for people to truly believe in us.

How To Win and Keep People's Confidence

Mistakes to Avoid

1. Be careful of your attitudes. These show in your expressions, tone of voice and behavior. Some of the most destructive of confidence are
   - being superior to others, too self-sufficient or "perfect";
   - being extremely important and deserving of their respect;
   - being too smart or powerful to have to obey the rules;
   - being overly self-confident;
   - having too little self-confidence, being cowardly.
2. Be careful of your actions. Some common mistakes are
   - trying to impress people;
   - trying to deceive people about yourself;
   - allowing "natural" destructive reactions to dominate your behavior, such as defensiveness, fear, irritability, impatience or dislike;
   - failing to give people evidence of your abilities and integrity;
   - failing to adjust your behavior so that it is appropriate for the circumstances;
   - acting in ways which destroy people's confidence in your motives or abilities (It is better to say and do nothing than to make matters worse).

3. Be realistic in your expectations. For example, do not assume that people will have confidence in you. This is natural because you see yourself in a favorable light. Others may be more conscious of your weaknesses.

Do not assume that people will have confidence in you because of your position or accomplishments. Many times people will *show* respect, a form of politeness, without actually *feeling* any respect.

Do not expect other people to always be fair in their attitudes toward you. Some individuals think no one can be trusted, including you. Others have unreasonable expectations of people; for them, a person is either totally perfect or totally imperfect. If you disappoint such people in even a small way, confidence is immediately withdrawn.

Others may form unfair or inaccurate opinions of you. They may jump to conclusions based upon their limited personal experience or the biased statements of others. They may be annoyed by some minor trait of yours or disappointed that you are not the kind of person they hoped you would be. They may get the impression that you are trying to impress them. All of these things will destroy confidence, even if the underlying opinions are unjustified.

Positive Steps To Take
1. To win respect for your abilities, give people evidence of them. Show what you can do by actually doing it. Do excellent work. Volunteer for hard assignments. Show initiative. Find problems and solve them; find opportunities and develop them. Go beyond what is required.

When speaking with people, say things that reveal your knowledge and understanding. Ask good questions. Reveal ways in which you agree with the others. Show an interest in them and in the things they find interesting.

Spend time with people. Do things with them. Help them with their projects. Arrange for mutually satisfying activities, the more emotionally positive, the better.

Display traits that people admire; speak and act in ways that they approve, especially where their interests are involved.

2. To win trust in your motives, give people evidence of them. Seek out opportunities to demonstrate your good intentions. Act in ways that others would approve, even at the expense of some of your own wants. Remind yourself that your long-range interests are best served by helping others as well as yourself. Prove that you will always stand on your principles by doing so in times of stress.

Be concerned with preserving and promoting the good of others. To show your concern, give them a hand, watch out for their interests, be tolerant of their wants and opinions, be sincere, honest, helpful and fair.

3. Be consistent in your performance; exercise patience. Consistency is important because people must come to firmly believe that you will do as they want and expect. One or two demonstrations of ability or reliability can be dismissed as "luck." Repeated evidence will be needed to establish the belief, "She definitely can do this and I can count on her."

4. Exhibit reasonable self-confidence and a reassuring attitude.

A proper degree of self-confidence is expected of anyone who is truly capable and reliable. A reassuring attitude will help doubters overcome their fears.

SUMMARY

Confidence in your motives and abilities (trust and respect) do not exist unless they are created. To do so, avoid saying and doing things that will destroy confidence. Instead, give people evidence of your abilities and motives through actual performance. Be consistent in demonstrating your desire and ability to help others.

APPLICATIONS

Create mutual confidence within a group by (1) having people work together on projects, and (2) encouraging an atmosphere of mutual trust. People perform much better when good performance is expected, as many research projects have shown. People will work to meet the expectations of their leaders and themselves.

A practice you might consider for your business is to initially trust everyone, that is, have confidence in others as a matter of policy. Treat people as if you had full faith in them. Then, use appropriate measures to protect yourself from those who betray your confidence. For the rest, your demonstration of faith in them can inspire a motivation to perform well, faith in themselves and each other, and an excellent group feeling.

You can create self-confidence in yourself or in another person by applying the principles of this chapter. Instead of just trying to talk yourself into feeling confident, win your own confidence by demonstrating to yourself what you can do. Put yourself into situations where you achieve the success you want. If you do this repeatedly, you will come to the *justified* conclusion, "I can do it." Gaining self-confidence utilizes the same process as winning the confidence of others.

81

Arrange the appropriate conditions for anyone who needs to develop more self-confidence. Assign tasks where he is challenged and uses his abilities in order to succeed. Present a succession of increasing challenges which develop his skills and increase self-assurance.

EXAMPLES

1. "I am a junior employee in a large company. I would like to become a supervisor and eventually a unit manager, but I cannot get anyone to give me a chance. I have no supervisory experience, so they say I am not qualified for a supervisory position. How can I demonstrate management ability if they will not let me manage anything?"
What is your answer?

Discussion: This sounds like an impossible situation, but it is not. There are several approaches this employee could take. First, she could find ways to work with the managers above her. This would provide an opportunity for them to see her at work and learn of her abilities first hand. Perhaps she could volunteer to work on a committee or project where superiors would notice her.

Second, she could find specific actions which would be considered good evidence of management ability. For example, she could complete a management degree or training program in her spare time. She could become expert in some aspect of the business, then apply her knowledge to solve problems and initiate programs in that area. She could volunteer for outside assignments, such as organizing the annual staff picnic, doing social or charity work in the community, or leading a sports team.

Third, she could tell her superiors of her ambitions and ask them what she needs to do to earn a promotion. She should then do those things most impressive to management in considering an employee for greater responsibility.

Fourth, she could ask for a trial period in supervision. She might become assistant to one of the present supervisors, substitute for one who was on vacation, or supervise a special project.

2. "How can we win the confidence of the banks in our plan for a new business? We need to borrow $200,000 from them to get it started."
What is your answer?

Discussion: Banks judge a loan application on the basis of profitability and the probability of repayment. The ability and motivation of the applicant is an important part of this judgement. They will look at your record of borrowing in the past, including how much you have borrowed and how well you paid. They will then look at your other assets and income, to judge your ability to pay if the business itself fails. They will estimate the likelihood that the new business will succeed by evaluating you, your business plan, and any other people or organizations involved in the undertaking.

To win their confidence, give them evidence of your business ability and your reliability in keeping promises. Give them evidence of your motivation to succeed. Present a well-reasoned plan to demonstrate your organizational skill and the reasons for your confidence in the new business. Gain the support of people who already have the bankers' confidence, perhaps by making them backers or partners in your new enterprise.

3. "Why do some people naturally win everybody's confidence and others do not? Are there techniques that can be learned?"
What is your answer?

Discussion: Some people are more inspiring of confidence because of their appearance, manner, position, personality, contacts, knowledge or any number of other factors. It may be difficult to emulate these. There are other traits that inspire confidence, however, including patterning your behavior to mirror that of the other person, showing a keen interest in him, and being a good listener. These techniques can be learned.

CHAPTER 9

ATTRACTING FAVORABLE ATTENTION

Sometimes we must deliberately attract people's attention. Reasons would include the need to bring a problem or danger to people's attention forcefully enough that they will act upon it, to communicate important information, to attract customers to our products or services, and to create the kind of personal image we wish to project. Other times, we need to change the attention we are attracting from unfavorable to favorable. Finally, since attention is anyone's first conscious reaction to a stimulus, we must gain their attention if we want people to act.

Causes of Attention

"Attention" refers to the process of becoming aware of something. Attention is selective: some objects are excluded from awareness at the same time that others are admitted. To pay attention is to place oneself in a condition which enhances the propensity to respond to certain stimuli, or to "set" oneself to respond to them.

Attention is automatically drawn to whatever has power to attract it. Attractions include external events detected through the senses and internal events such as thoughts, feelings and memories.

Certain happenings almost always capture attention. These include whatever is

- intense, as a loud noise or bright light;
- moving or changing;
- repeated over and over;
- isolated; standing out from its surroundings;
- asymmetrical or irregular;
- novel; surprising;
- incongruous; unusual;
- complex;
- highly similar to something else.

The state of the observer can affect attention. A hungry person may notice the smell of food faster. You will notice a new item if it reminds you strongly of something familiar. Being interested in a topic helps you pay attention to it.

Attention has its limitations. One is the relative strength of attention attractors. For example, children, pets and television programs are strong attention attractors. They will distract people from almost any other stimulus.

Time is another limitation. We can retain a single item in consciousness for only a few seconds. When attention is to be held longer, there must be a sequence of related items passing through our awareness.

Our control over attention is limited by the fact that it is largely involuntary. (Imagine deciding not to hear a telephone when it rings.) The involuntary nature of attention makes it a good defensive mechanism: it "makes" us notice those things most likely to harm us.

Another limit on attention is fatigue. The longer we concentrate on one thing, the less novel it becomes. Distractors grow relatively more attractive. Eventually, fatigue will stop all attention (We fall asleep).

How To Attract Favorable Attention

What To Avoid Doing:

The most frequent mistake is simply not thinking about how another person's attention is to be attracted and held. We may assume that because we are attentive and interested, others will be too. We may become so absorbed with our own purposes that we fail to notice signs of inattention in others.

The nature of attention as a defense mechanism means that negative features tend to have a greater impact than positive ones. Our undesirable features may be gaining more notice than our good ones. Therefore, we should avoid unattractive appearance, unpleasant manner of speech, annoying behaviors and unappealing attitudes. We will gain favorable attention only when we provide generally positive experiences for others.

Our habits can cause problems. If we always act and talk the same way, we may fail to keep people's attention because our behavior has become too familiar.

We may inadvertently divert people's attention away from matters we wish them to notice. We may speak in a monotone. We may have distracting mannerisms. We may confuse people, especially if our presentations are not organized well enough to make important points stand out. Poor interpersonal relations may cause people to dwell upon thoughts which are not the ones we wish them to have.

Finally, physical and psychological conditions may not have received enough of our consideration. A room which is too hot, stuffy, noisy, busy, crowded, empty or poorly arranged will distract attention from the subject being discussed. People who are worried about other matters, tired, daydreaming, or emotionally upset will find it difficult to pay attention.

What To Do Instead:

1. Enhance the attention potential of those features you want people to notice by linking them with natural attention attractors. Make the important points more intense than others. For example, make changes, repeat important ideas, present them in an unusual way, introduce variety in your presentation style, and be more dramatic.

2. Reduce the attraction potential of those items which you do not wish people to notice or which might distract them from the desired attractors. Remove noises, extraneous activity, obstructions, and annoyances. Do not associate negative features with any natural attention attractors. To accomplish this, do not talk about the negative features, color them the same as the background, or surround them with items of no importance.

3. When presenting ideas, use proven techniques such as these:

- Show Contrast and Similarity.

Point out how one item is strikingly different from another. Contrast what used to be with what is now, what people believe with the actual facts, or what we are doing with what we should be doing. Use similarity: draw parallels between one set of ideas or occurrences and another.

- Arouse Interest and Curiosity.

Relate what you have to say to the interests of the audience. Arouse curiosity by getting people to ask themselves questions about the topic. Sustain curiosity by keeping them wondering what is coming next; do not tell them everything or answer all their questions too soon.

However, do not count on interest and curiosity to retain attention if all other causes of attention are absent. You must still use attention attractors.

- Make Pleasing and Satisfying Statements.

You employ this technique whenever you show an interest in a person, treat him as a valuable individual, ask his advice, compliment him or express appreciation for what he has done. Flattery can gain favorable attention. Honest praise is even better.

- Make Threatening or Challenging Statements.

People quickly give attention to anything that may endanger them, throw their competence into question, reveal that they have been wrong, impose unwelcome regulations or restrictions, or make them lose face. Although effective, these methods can backfire. They tend to arouse ill feeling and should be used only as a last resort.

4. You can create a favorable personal image by attracting the right kind of attention. Your image consists of those features which are most striking and memorable to

others. These may not be the ones you would like them to see. Find out how people react to you now. Then, decide which features you wish to have them notice and those you do not. Use the methods discussed to enhance the former and disguise the latter.

For example, if you wish to appear more mature, you should eliminate behavior characteristic of younger people. This might include high physical activity level, impatience, speaking and believing naively, and dressing in young fashions. Emphasize the characteristics of a mature person, such as a calmer and more reasoned manner of speech, clothes and grooming typical of adults, more mature interests and patience.

After making these changes, check again to see if people react the way you had hoped. Some attempts to project an image do not work at all. A very young person acting too "grown up" can look silly, as can an older person "acting like a kid." Adjust your strategy until you are successful. One highly effective method is to imitate the behavior of people who already project the image you desire.

5. Promote your product or services by gaining favorable attention. Borrow some of the techniques used by advertisers. Make your message striking and memorable. Make the main benefits to the customer stand out. Keep it as short as possible while still getting the message across.

Create a good company image by featuring the favorable aspects of the business. An organization could be portrayed as reliable, innovative, providing excellent service, a good corporate citizen, an excellent place to work, a sound investment, or in any number of other ways.

Use positive features to offset undesirable ones. For example, you could contribute to visible improvements in your community. This might make up for negative factors, such as factory noise or poor building appearance. Practice good public relations: draw attention to the good things you do.

Be sure to promote your organization among your own employees, as well. If they feel pride in the company, they will become your most effective good-will ambassadors.

SUMMARY

Attention is an automatic response. Use attention attractors to feature those things you wish people to notice. Remove attention attractors from unfavorable items. Apply attention-gaining methods for effective communication, bringing matters forcefully into people's awareness, creating a desired personal image, and promoting the organization and its products.

APPLICATIONS

Books on sales and marketing contain many examples of the effective use of attention attractors. One such book describes an insurance salesman who gained attention of prospects by the expensive, custom-made clothes he wore. Another tells of a sales manager who became famous for his dramatic presentations. (He once started a meeting by suddenly pulling out a revolver and firing it at the ceiling.)

Marketing campaigns provide many other good examples. To create an image of competence and success, one company required all sales and service personnel to wear white shirts and blue blazers. Another company used pink luxury cars to dramatize its sales force. This reinforced its desired image of a glamorous lifestyle, which it wanted customers to associate with its products.

On the management level, attention techniques can be used in

- getting employees to notice (and take seriously) problems, dangers, new procedures, regulations and other communications from management;
- making the top managers realize that a problem is serious enough to warrant their action;
- causing people to notice products and services and to respond favorably;
- having others see *you* as an effective leader.

EXAMPLES

1. "We are the newest auto parts distributor in town. The market here is 'mature,' the various products are very similar, and our competition is well-entrenched. How can we get the kind of favorable attention we need to make a go of it?"
What is your answer?

Discussion: The new distributor must be different from the competition in some way. Management should decide which differences give them the best chance of success. For instance, they might decide to become the lowest-cost supplier in the area. This would be a good strategy if the older distributors were charging too much or the new company could cut costs below the others. They would then develop a marketing plan around this strategy.

Attention would then be drawn to their best feature, low cost, by choice of an appropriate company name. They might call themselves "Budget Auto Parts" or "Economy Automotive Supplies," for example. Their advertising, sales training, promotional material and company organization would all be designed to reinforce the desired image.

If low-cost was not the best strategy, other possibilities are fast delivery, large inventory, long hours, free credit, personal service, or any desirable feature. To suggest personal service and reliability, the owner's name could be used in the company title – as in "Johnson Auto Parts." This would be most effective if the owner was well-known among potential customers.

Specializing to satisfy an unmet customer need will give this business the best chance for breaking into the market.

2. "How can I attract favorable attention from upper management and others so I can further my career?"
What is your answer?

Discussion: This person needs to do three things: (1) attract attention, (2) make sure that the attention is favorable, and (3) attract the favorable attention of the right people, namely, superiors who can help him advance.

Here are some approaches to try:

- work well and hope that good performance will be noticed;
- volunteer for tough assignments and do a spectacular job on them;

- take extra training; become extremely well-qualified;
- prepare thoroughly, then speak out intelligently at management and training meetings;
- develop many acquaintances throughout the organization;
- demonstrate high motivation by the amount of work done;
- select a particular manager and gain his personal attention by working with him (gaining a "mentor");
- anything else that makes him different, makes him stand out enough to attract attention, creates a favorable impression, is useful to the organization, and indicates his further potential.

3. "In addition to frequent reports to management, I make sales presentations to clients and talks to trade groups. Would I be more effective if I made a deliberate effort to attract their attention? How could this be done without appearing obvious or foolish?"
What is your answer?

Discussion: All communication must be tailored to its audience. If your audience would think a dramatic gesture foolish or obvious, then, clearly, you do not want to do it.

Still, you can find ways to organize your presentations and illustrate your points that will help listeners understand the principal ideas. A leading statement is most noticeable, for example. You will want to put important items in this position. Use visual illustrations: it is easier to comprehend something that is seen as well as heard. Dramatic flair helps hold attention. Use it to whatever extent you can (without overdoing it).

People find it easier to pay attention when the speed of presentation is neither too slow nor too fast. They can pay attention better if they are actively involved, as in discussions or practice exercises.

Vary your tone of voice, move around, have another person speak, show pictures, ask questions – anything that introduces variety and makes the message stand out.

Spoken reports are frequently judged more by the impression made by the speaker than the content of the presentation. Pay special attention to how you "come across" to your audience.

4. "I am in charge of the company motor pool. We attract unfavorable attention whenever we do not deliver a vehicle on schedule. These instances are usually not our fault — someone brought the car back late or it broke down unexpectedly — but we get the blame. How can I diminish this unfavorable attention and get people to notice how well we perform most of the time?"
What is your answer?

Discussion: Use positive aspects of your service to draw attention away from these unavoidable problems. One way would be to call the next user as soon as you saw that there might be a delay. Call again as the scheduled time approaches. This will show your concern for the person who is waiting and demonstrate that you are doing your best to provide the vehicle. His attention is drawn away from the negative feature (no car available) to the positive one (your efforts and concern for him).

An even more effective method would be to eliminate the negative attention attractors. Institute procedures which will prevent problems. Require vehicles to be returned well before the next appointment, so there will be time to do something if they are late. Keep a vehicle or two in reserve or have a back-up arrangement with a car-rental agency. You could also warn all users that problems sometimes arise and explain the procedure for helping them in such a case.

CHAPTER 10

GAINING
COOPERATION

Gaining cooperation is probably the most important of the leadership skills.

All organizations are built on cooperation. It is far more practical than competition or isolated individual effort. In cooperation, we help each other; in competition, we interfere with each other and destroy each others' efforts; as isolated individuals, we work inefficiently.

Cooperation is so effective that we pass laws against its use in certain circumstances. For instance, if large corporations cooperate to eliminate free competition, they may become so successful that they can control the market and take advantage of customers instead of serving them.

Anytime conflict, competition or isolated individual effort are changed to cooperation, amazing increases in performance are realized. This is especially true for converting conflict to cooperation. We save the energy we were using before to defend ourselves and overcome obstacles devised by our competitors. Having gained their help, we can accomplish even more.

When you gain employees' willing cooperation, you do not have to force them to do what you want. Work becomes easier and more pleasant for everyone. People enjoy what they are doing, have better interpersonal relations, and are more motivated. Group performance improves as a result.

The Nature of Cooperation

Cooperation means people working together for a common goal. It is a joint effort, coordinated so that each helps the others. With cooperation, people work willingly because *each* will benefit from accomplishment of the common goal.

Cooperation is not the same as obedience. When people obey you, even willingly, their goal is always different from yours. For example, suppose you order the dock crew to unload a semi-trailer by 4:00 P.M. and they obey you. Why do they obey? Their reason is to keep from being fired, to live up to their labor contract, because they like you, or for some other similar reason. These reasons are *not* the same as your's or the company's. You want the trailer unloaded in time to meet production schedules, reduce costs or accomplish other organizational objectives.

True cooperation would result if the crew had the same specific goal as the company. The workers would want to unload by 4:00 P.M. if they received a bonus for producing a cost reduction, or got to go home early if the production schedule were met. Then, their goal and the organization's would be the same.

People need not receive the same benefit from achievement of a common goal, but the goal must be wanted by all.

Mistakes To Avoid:

Attitudes can interfere with cooperation.

Because of cultural traditions glorifying "rugged individualism," some people think that cooperating is a sign of weakness. Others regard life as a constant battle, with the best man or woman winning only through ruthless competition.

Many do not recognize the practicality of cooperative action. Authoritarian attitudes, such as enjoyment of exercising power over others, can interfere. Cooperation is not realized then because no effort is made to obtain it, or because others actively resist.

Actions can hurt cooperation.

The most serious error is threatening, criticizing, ordering or pressuring those whose cooperation is desired. Pressure creates resistance and fear, which may be a way to get obedience but certainly not cooperation.

If you try to gain both cooperation and obedience – using persuasion and the threat of force at the same time – the result will be to confuse people. Each method interferes with the other.

We make mistakes when we do not know what is required for joint effort, have not developed our skills as leaders, think only of ourselves, fail to win the confidence of others, create ill will, communicate poorly or lose control of our emotions.

Finally, you cannot win cooperation unless you give it in return.

How To Gain Cooperation

Cooperation exists almost automatically if the causal conditions are right. Otherwise, it is virtually impossible to achieve.

Therefore, your objective should be to create and maintain the conditions needed for cooperation.

Conditions For Cooperation:

1. Each person involved must have an opportunity to benefit by his efforts and by the achievement of the goal;
2. These benefits must be apparent to each person;
3. Each person must judge the benefits to be worth the time, effort, and other resources he must contribute;
4. Each must judge the benefits received and the contributions made by all to be fair (or fair enough); no one may gain a disproportionate amount of the rewards or contribute a less-than-reasonable amount of the costs;
5. Each must have confidence in the plan, that it will succeed and will provide the anticipated rewards;
6. Each must have confidence in the other people, that they will do their part;
7. Each must understand his role, know (or be able to decide) exactly what to do, and be able to coordinate his actions with the others'.

These conditions assume that
- Participants' purposes are compatible;
- Interpersonal relations are good enough to allow people to work together;

- Threats and pressure are avoided (they distract from the underlying motives);
- There is an explicit or implicit agreement which specifies the objective, the plan, the contributions each is to make and the benefits each is to receive.

Steps To Take:

1. Examine your own motives to be sure you want cooperation and not just obedience. Be prepared to do what is necessary to achieve it.

2. Be sure conditions necessary for cooperation are present. If not, create them.

3. Develop a plan. Include the role each will play, the costs to each, the sequence of steps needed, and the benefits to each. The plan must be practical, realistic, believable and fair.

4. Persuade people to cooperate in the plan.
   - Gain their favorable attention and win their confidence, as needed.
   - Arouse their interest in the benefits to be realized.
   - Explain your plan and convince them that it would work.
   - Explain their part and convince them that their contributions would be adequately rewarded.
   - Get people involved in the planning and action; arouse enthusiasm for the project; get it underway as soon as possible.

5. Maintain cooperation throughout the project.

As time goes by, people may lose sight of the benefits, begin to doubt that the enterprise will be successful, lose confidence in the people involved, or feel that the rewards are no longer worth the costs. Their wants may change so that they no longer desire the benefits.

Watch for these problems, especially loss of enthusiasm. Find out what has gone wrong and correct it. Re-convince people that their continued cooperation will be well rewarded.

SUMMARY

Cooperation will exist if and only if the necessary conditions are present. These include the opportunity for each to benefit, a judgment that the costs are worth the rewards, a belief in the fairness of the plan, confidence in the program and the people, and a knowledge of what to do. Cooperation is not the same as obedience.

APPLICATIONS

1. List cooperation problems in your organization. These might include individuals who refuse to cooperate with you, groups that work together poorly, or departments that fail to help each other.

Analyze each of these situations for the presence of conditions necessary for cooperation. You should find that one or more is missing in each case.

Determine what steps could be taken to create the needed cooperative conditions. Plan how you would convince the people involved that their best interests will best be served by working together.

2. You may find that cooperation is not always the best method. It must be balanced by individual action.

For example, no one will join in a cooperative action if it is not in his best interest. Independent action or no action would be better than working against one's own good.

Some individuals seem to think that cooperating means that they do not have to do anything. They may believe that all they are expected to contribute is agreement with what the leaders do. However, cooperative action is still action, and it must be taken by each participant. There really is no such thing as "group action": a group acts only in so far as individuals within it act and coordinate those actions.

Learn to recognize when cooperation and when individual performance needs to be encouraged.

3. Do you know how to convert a competitive situation into a cooperative one?

In a competitive situation, one person loses whatever the other gains. There is an incompatibility of wants, so cooperation is *impossible* under these conditions.

To change such a situation, first remove the incompatibility of wants. The alternatives are these: (1) the first person gives up what he wants to help the other, (2) the other person gives up what she wants to help the former, (3) they agree to split or share the reward, or (4) both give up their goals and work on something else.

For example, suppose you and another individual want the same promotion. Your alternatives for cooperative action are (1) to allow your competitor to have the promotion in return for something he will help you attain, (2) to persuade him to give up the promotion to you in return for your help in gaining another goal for him (such as another promotion), (3) to see if the company would split the job so each of you could have part of it, or (4) to both abandon this promotion and work together on some other goal, such as starting a new division in which you would both become the top managers.

Consider another example. Suppose you have a serious labor-management disagreement over work rules and wages. You could convert the conflict situation into a cooperative one by finding ways for each side to gain significant goals while giving in return to the other. Wage increases might be tied to changes in work rules, productivity or profits. Employee stock ownership plans or participation in decision making might be exchanged for pay increases. If times are bad, job security and the survival of the company could be used as incentives.

Conflict will be resolved when you find a goal and a plan that both parties want enough to enter into an agreement, and when both become convinced that this is the best they can do under the circumstances.

EXAMPLES

1. "I am foreman in a plant which makes steel cabinets and shelves. One of the men, Charlie, keeps disrupting the work by trying to start arguments with me, slowing down the line, and finding things to complain about. He always does this when the other men can see and hear him, and he tries to get them to support him.

Management now wants me to institute new procedures for moving the welded pieces through the finishing sheds. This will require everyone to change some work habits. I am afraid Charlie will cause trouble over this. If he makes a fuss, the other workers may not cooperate either.

I cannot fire Charlie or move him. What can I do to get his cooperation?"

What is your answer?

Discussion: A solution to this problem will depend upon Charlie's motivation. Is Charlie just a troublemaker? Is he a show-off, trying to get attention? Does he have a personal grudge against the foreman?

From the description of his actions, it sounds like Charlie wants to be in charge himself. If this is so, then he is in a power struggle with the foreman. Each wants to be in control.

In this true incident, the foreman recognized Charlie's need for control and gave him an opportunity to share it in return for his help in introducing the new procedures. The foreman first explained the new methods to everyone. He turned to Charlie and said, "Charlie, I have some work to do at the other end of the plant. I want you to take charge here while I am gone and make sure these new procedures are done properly." Then, he left. When he returned an hour later, he found the men working smoothly under Charlie's direction. The new procedures were instituted without any problems.

Many foremen would hesitate to share authority this way, fearing they would lose control of the employees or would look like they were not doing their jobs. Of course, there is some danger of this happening. However, there are opportunities as well. A foreman with an eye to advancement realizes what a trained replacement would mean: he himself would be available for promotion when a position opened. Furthermore, he could use the time now available, because of having an assistant, to find and solve production problems. This, in turn, would make him more effective in his job, help the company, qualify him for suitable rewards, and consequently make his foreman's position even more secure.

A prime source of new first-line supervisors can be found in the natural leaders who emerge from among the workers. This group could include union representatives, if they were willing to advance into management.

2. "My duties in the police department require me to contact an officer in another section frequently. I must ask him to look up information which I need. He used to do this willingly, but recently he has been putting me off.

I am not trying to take advantage of him. I must have his help to do my job. How can I get his cooperation?"
What is your answer?

Discussion: For cooperation to exist, each person must have an opportunity to benefit. What benefits does the other officer in this case receive for cooperating? Either there are none, or the rewards are insufficient to overcome the inconvenience he must endure.

Therefore, the speaker needs to provide something of value in return for the assistance received. Possibilities would include

- giving the other officer credit for his help, for example, by arranging official recognition for the assistance (such as a letter to his supervisor), thanking him publicly, mentioning his help to other people, and thanking him personally;
- doing return favors, by finding ways to help him or providing other appropriate rewards;
- making friends with him, which would give him a reason to help (namely, as a favor for a friend);

- appealing to his sense of duty, perhaps by pointing out how much his assistance means to the success of the department or how important it is in achieving important results;
- reducing the inconvenience to him, organizing requests so that they are easier to fulfill;
- reaching an agreement with him on how you will work together; getting the best results with minimum inconvenience for each.

Some might be tempted to use authority to solve this problem. They would have the other officer's superior order him to do as requested. Except as a last resort, this would be a poor approach. (It would mean involving superiors in a situation which should be solved by the people directly involved. It would then appear that this officer cannot handle his job or cannot work well with others. It would probably make the other officer angry and, subsequently, even less inclined to cooperate.)

3. "I am newly promoted to supervisor of my department. I am authorized to make all necessary changes to bring the section up to standard.

I am having trouble with two former co-workers who are now subordinates. They resent the fact that I was promoted over them and argue with me on any move I want to make.

I would like to rearrange the work schedule. This will increase efficiency, but will also mean changing everyone's hours.

How can I get my former co-workers to cooperate with me on this?"

What is your answer?

Discussion: Promotion is often accompanied by transfer in order to avoid problems like these. The long-term solution, which is to win their confidence and reduce their resentment, does not help at this present time.

The supervisor might try asking for their cooperation on the basis of fairness. (Most people want to feel they are being fair.) She could indicate her desire to help them in return for their cooperation. She could offer them specific favors, such as choice of assignment or shift. (This could be dangerous, however, because it shows favoritism over other workers.) She could bargain with them, and the others, for their assistance. She could try to persuade them to work together for the good of the company.

If all these methods failed, the new supervisor might have to resort to force. She could take away some of their benefits. She could give them the choice of straightening up or leaving. If they still refused to cooperate, no matter what she did, she may have to terminate some or all of them. (Losing all control would mean her failure as a supervisor.)

After a confrontation with authority, people will sometimes change their attitudes and become cooperative. They may have been testing the new supervisor or expressing their frustrations. When the confrontation is over, they no longer feel a need to cause trouble because they have had their say.

4. "Like every executive I know, I must frequently take work home from the office. The problem is that my wife and children will not leave me alone so I can do it. The kids are after me to play with them or read to them or fix something. My wife expects me to run errands, help

around the house, entertain her friends or go out.

My career is very important to me. I have to do this evening work or I will probably not succeed.

How can I get my family's cooperation?"
What is your answer?

Discussion: A family conference is in order here. The man must find out if his wife and children understand why he brings work home in the evening and if they agree with his reasons for doing so. He should explain the benefits to them, if there are any.

An agreement might be reached with the children in which he agrees to pay attention to them during certain times in return for being allowed to work in peace at other times. Special rewards could be given for their cooperation, such as trips to ball games or movies.

He could give his wife some rewards in return for her help, as well. She may be happy to cooperate if she sees that something desirable (for her) will result from his business success.

On the other hand, his family might not agree that his job is so important that he should bring it home every night. In that case, he will have to compromise with them on how much of his time should be spent on office work and how much on family matters. He might give up some of the time he wants for business projects in return for their giving up some of the time they feel he should be devoting to them.

Compromise is the key to settling problems where each party has legitimate interests but all cannot be satisfied at once. Without compromise, one side would always be taking advantage of the other. This would lead to unhappiness and worse problems in the future.

5. "My employer encourages us to get involved in community activities, so I volunteered to become a scout leader. My problem is lack of cooperation from the parents. I need help in planning and putting on meetings, taking field trips, and going with the scouts to summer camp. Every time I ask, the parents say they have some conflict.

How can I get their cooperation?"
What is your answer?

Discussion: Once people become used to receiving a service without having to contribute, they will resist efforts to change the arrangement. The former scout leaders had probably been doing all the work for the troop. If the parents never had to help before, they will resist it now.

Here are two approaches to try. First, get the parents to agree to help when their child first joins the group. This creates a contract or promise that they will later feel obligated to honor.

Second, provide benefits to the parents who do help. For example, give them credit through public recognition of their contributions. Schedule activities that will naturally appeal to adults, such as picnics or canoe trips. Have recognition ceremonies for the scouts: the parents will want to participate because of pride in their children. Ask parents to conduct a program on a topic of interest to them or an area of their expertise. Create good feelings of friendship and appreciation among the adults who assist the group.

These methods may not gain everyone's help, but the right combination should win over enough parents to gain the needed cooperation.

CHAPTER 11

MAKING YOURSELF CLEARLY UNDERSTOOD

The Importance of Successful Communication

Failure of communication causes many of the problems between people. One type of failure is *miscommunication* which occurs whenever people think you mean one thing but you really mean something else. For example, people may become angry or resentful if they mistakenly think you are insulting them; they may do a job incorrectly if they misunderstand what you want; they may resist your suggestions if they misinterpret your motives.

Other problems are caused by a simple *lack of communication,* when people do not receive the information they need. If they are unaware of vital information, they cannot make sound decisions.   If they know nothing of the organization's plans, they cannot cooperate or feel a part of the team. If they fail to understand the reasons for your suggestions, they may resist them.

Communication ability is one of the most important of the leadership skills. As a leader, you must effectively explain decisions and plans, clearly express the views and values of the group, relate the group goals to each person's individual efforts, and represent the organization well to outside groups.

Requirements of Successful Communication

We say we communicate by "giving" or "sharing" our thoughts or by "transmitting information." These are not literally true. They are figurative descriptions of the actual process.

When we communicate successfully, we cause the intended receiver to have an idea. This idea must be similar enough to the idea we wanted him to have that our purpose in communicating is accomplished.

For example, if you tell a shoe salesperson, "I want to try on those loafers," and she brings you the shoes you wanted, then you have communicated successfully, even if the shoes are not really called "loafers." The idea she formed was close enough to the idea you wanted her to have to accomplish your goal, namely, of trying those particular shoes.

The steps involved in successful communication are as follows:

1. You form an idea which you want to communicate to the other person;

2. You encode the idea, by representing it in a recognized system of symbols such as words or pictures;

3. You create a pattern of sound vibrations in the air

(speak), or create a visual image, or otherwise direct an energy pattern toward the intended receiver;

4. The receiver responds to the energy pattern, recognizes it as a code, decodes it, and forms an idea as a result. If this resulting idea is similar to the one you wanted him or her to have, you have communicated successfully.

The causal conditions necessary for communication include these:

1. The sender must formulate a clear and consistent idea;

2. The sender must express this idea well, in language or other recognizable code;

3. The sender must transmit the coded message in a way that it is receivable and decodable by the receiver; the symbol system (code) must "mean" the same to sender and receiver;

4. The receiver must receive, recognize and decode the message successfully;

5. Sender and receiver must want to understand each other;

6. Each must attract attention and pay attention enough for the process to take place.

We cannot show others directly what ideas are in our minds. Therefore, we must use symbols. Symbols are anything that stands for or represents something else.

The nature of symbols and symbol systems implies certain additional conditions for successful communication, as follows:

1. Anything can be used as symbols. We commonly use words, gestures, objects, actions, noises, postures, motions, forms, colors, facial expressions, tones, printed or written characters, clothing or lack of clothing, drawings, diagrams, graphs, paintings, sculpture, the presence or absence of something, and many other devices.

2. Words in a language have two types of meaning. First is the *connotative* meaning which is given by a definition equating the word with other words, as in a dictionary. Connotative meanings allow us to learn new ideas based on ideas we already have. We do not have to experience everything first-hand, which would be impossible, anyway. Second is *denotative* meaning, which is the object or state of affairs to which the word refers (points). For example, a road sign with the word "Bump" refers to or points to a bump in the road ahead. Denotative meanings allow us to connect symbols to the real world.

3. When people speak of "The Meaning" of an expression, they usually have in mind the *customary* meaning. This is the meaning taught in schools, given in dictionaries, and most frequently intended when the expression is used. It is the "correct" meaning. Even so, there is no law that compels anyone to use a word or expression in the customary way. You can use the word to mean anything you want. (Of course, if you use it in unusual ways, people will have difficulty understanding you. You may even have trouble keeping your thoughts clear!)

Whatever you plan to communicate, you will do best if you use customary meanings. People are more likely to understand you if you do. On the other hand, customary usage may be inadequate for expressing new ideas. If you can convey these more effectively using different symbols, as a creative artist might do, then novel methods of expression could be better.

4. Common languages and symbol systems cannot express all the connotations and implications which are part of your ideas. When you encode them, you also impoverish them to some extent. This is not necessarily bad. It forces you to leave out unessential meanings that

might just confuse the receiver. If the message achieves your communication goal, then you have succeeded, even if the message is incomplete or imperfect in some ways.

People choose words in order to express and convey their ideas. These words are generally used with the meaning customarily assigned to them in the language system. However, this need not be so. For every particular use of language, *a word or expression means whatever the person using it wants it to mean and wishes to express by it.*

Therefore, your job, as sender or receiver, is to concentrate on the underlying meaning, that meaning which the other person has in mind and is trying to communicate.

Causes of Misunderstanding

Many mistakes occur because we fail to understand the nature of communication or fail to create the conditions necessary for it to occur. For example:

1. We may not allow for necessary thinking by
   - failing to allow enough time;
   - trying to tell people our opinions instead of allowing them to think for themselves;
   - failing to arouse their desire to think about the topic;
   - expecting them to consider things completely beyond their experience;
   - not recognizing when there is resistance to thinking, because of reluctance to disturb cherished beliefs, having to admit error, or having to change behavior.

2. We may not encode a message properly. We may
- not have thought the matter through thoroughly enough before beginning to speak;
- use poor expression or organization;
- forget that the symbols we use could have different meanings for others;
- not realize that our tone of voice and facial expression, or the context and occasion of communication, can change the perceived meanings of our words;
- fail to find out if our receivers are really understanding us;
- assume that we have communicated successfully just because we were thinking about what we meant at the same time we were speaking.

Mistakes in communication are often caused by mistakes in thinking.

3. We may let interpersonal feelings interfere. We might
- not have the person's confidence;
- not really care if he understands;
- be distracted by worry, anger, fear, suspicion, personal dislikes or other negative emotions;
- have a fundamental disagreement with our receiver in matters of values or philosophy of life;
- place on the other person the full responsibility for understanding;
- become upset when others do not respond as we want.

4. We may assume that conflicts always arise from a clash of interests or wants. Actually, interpersonal conflicts are frequently due to misunderstandings.

A good policy to adopt is this: approach every conflict as if it were a misunderstanding. Then, if it really is a misunderstanding, you can solve the problem easily. If it is a conflict of wants after all, you have still greatly increased your chances for working out a cooperative solution by not "coming on too strong" at the start, and by showing a desire to understand the other person.

Increasing Your Communications Skills

Step #1:

The first step in any plan is to decide on your objective. In the case of communication, you have two objectives to consider:

1. The general objective in all communication is to obtain understanding by causing the receiver to have the desired idea.

This is *not* the same thing as causing the person to accept or believe the idea. (That process is called "convincing.") *Gaining understanding and getting agreement are not the same thing. Understanding must always come first.*

Therefore, *never try to get agreement before you have gained understanding.* At this stage, do not argue on any point. If the other person says he disagrees with you, steer the conversation back to your prime objective of gaining understanding. Say, "Let's be sure we both understand this point before trying to decide whether it is right or wrong," or "Why don't I finish my explanation of the process first; then we'll discuss it?"

2. The specific purpose of a communication should be made as clear as possible before communication is begun. You will need to know the answers to these questions:

- What is my purpose in communicating? Why am I trying to get understanding? (Is it business or pleasure? Am I trying for a specific result or just passing the time? Is it a game or is it serious? ...)
- What exactly do I want this person to be able to *do*

once he understands? (To run the machine, repair it, paint it, appraise it or what?)

- How will I know if he has understood? (Will I give him a quiz? Will I see if he does the job right? Will I ask him questions?)
- How can I make my message most easily understood by this particular person, without distorting its meaning?

Step #2:

Plan your communication to include the following:

1. Consideration of the Receiver

Take into account the age, sex, family background, experience, education, level of knowledge, opinions, values, interests, temperament, position and language habits of your audience. Think about the communication from the receivers' point of view. Make your message something they will be able and willing to comprehend.

2. Preparation of the Message

Decide precisely what you want the recipient to know and be able to do. Clarify your goal in your own mind.

Organize the message to progress in a logical, easy-to-follow sequence. Make important points stand out by placing them at points of emphasis.

Select examples, illustrations, demonstrations, displays, discussion questions and similar devices which will help receivers understand how the general principles apply in familiar situations. Ideally, every general statement will be illustrated by an example.

If this is a personal presentation, decide how you will act. The attitudes you project will mean as much to your audience as anything you say. They will "read" your attitudes in your expressions, tone of voice, posture, dress and the way you formulate your ideas. Also consider your relationships with the receivers, the circumstances of the communication, the other persons' wants and feelings, and your motives toward them.

Decide in advance how you will handle problems. What will you do if the audience is indifferent, bored, hostile, suspicious, argumentative, or rejecting of everything you say?

Be prepared to modify or even abandon your communication plan if necessary. Have alternative plans ready to go.

Step #3:
During communication, concentrate on these objectives:
1. Keep conditions favorable for understanding.

Choose the proper time and place. For a group meeting, important factors are the size of the room, lighting, ventilation, acoustics, and arrangement of furniture. Eliminate distractions such as noise and anything which may cause discomfort.

Avoid actions which anger, offend, bore, alienate or otherwise cause receivers to lose their desire to understand you.

Do not "lecture" or "preach." Win and keep people's confidence. Maintain a friendly spirit of cooperation.
2. Lead your receivers to think.

Do not just "tell" them: urge them to think about what you say. Remember, it is only through their own thinking that they can come to understand.

Some other points to remember:
- People think about what comes into their attention. Therefore, use the methods for capturing and holding it.

- People think about what they want and things that arouse their interest. Therefore, relate what you have to say to their wants. Make your presentation interesting.
- Thinking can be initiated and directed by questions. Therefore, arouse curiosity about your topic so the audience asks itself questions. Pose questions as part of your presentations.
- Repetition helps people notice and remember. Therefore, use repetition of main points.
- A message is more likely to get through if it is sent more than one way. Therefore, use two or more media to express ideas. For example, tell them and show them, write a letter and follow it with a telephone call, present your report orally and again in writing.
- Adjust your behavior as you go along. Learn from experience what methods work for you. Practice to develop your skills.

3. Find out if your intended receivers have understood. If not, modify your communication accordingly. Watch your audience for signs of confusion or boredom. Ask questions which will reveal the depth of their comprehension. Encourage them to ask you questions. Use discussion to reveal ambiguities and misunderstandings.

For written materials, have someone read what you have written before final distribution. Ask them questions to find out if they understood what you meant. Test all important communications in a similar fashion *before* presentation.

No matter how well you prepare and explain, people can and will often misunderstand you. Test the effectiveness of your message. It is up to you to find out if your receivers "got the message." (If they did not, adjust your methods and try again.)

SUMMARY

Miscommunication is the reason for many problems between people. Successful communication occurs when we cause the intended receiver to have the ideas we wish him to have. Causal conditions necessary for successful communication include attention, a desire to think about the message and ability to understand it. Planning communication is essential. It should include clear conception of the objective to be obtained, consideration of the receivers, good formulation, favorable conditions, leading receivers to think and finding out if they have understood. Good communicators assume responsibility for their results and practice to improve their skills.

APPLICATIONS

1. Analyze your organization. What are the major communications problems? What are their causes? What could be done to correct them?

2. Analyze your job. What are the primary communications needs? What are the inherent problems? How should these be handled?

3. Analyze your abilities. What are your strongest communication abilities? How can you take advantage of them? What are your communication weaknesses? How can you correct or offset them?

4. Select a real situation in which you must communicate successfully. Plan how you will do it. Include considera-

tion of the setting, the receivers, the message to be conveyed, the emotional tone and other factors which may affect literal meaning, examples to be used, organization of the message, how to help receivers understand and remember the main points, and any follow-up needed.

EXAMPLES

1. "I am in charge of a road crew. I tell these guys to do something — sometimes I tell them a hundred times! — but they are just too dumb to understand anything.

I have fired a lot of these dumbbells, but the new ones are always just as bad.

How can I get these stupid jerks to understand a simple order?"
What is your answer?

Discussion: This crew foreman is placing full responsibility for communication and understanding on his employees. Chances are good that he is phrasing his orders poorly and putting little thought into them. Furthermore, his negative attitude toward the workers is probably very clear to them. This would cause resentment and resistance toward him and a lack of any desire to understand him.

The first step toward solving this problem will be taken when the foreman himself accepts responsibility for successfully communicating with the workers, even if they are as "dumb" as he says. (The less ability your receivers have, the more *you* must clarify the ideas for them.)

Specific steps the foreman could take would include
- training of all employees in the terms and methods used in the work;
- training some employees ("straw bosses") to understand the foreman and pass his instructions along to the others, by showing them or otherwise;
- reformulating the foreman's orders into pictures, demonstrations, or other symbols the workers can understand.

2. "In my company, all communication comes from the top down. We get orders constantly. We spend our time following orders and filling out reports. We never get to think for ourselves, even if we know a better way.

Whenever we want to tell management about our needs or problems, or make suggestions, the communication is blocked from above or it is just ignored.

Why does this company permit only one-way communication? Why won't management listen to us? How can we get through to them?"
What is your answer?

Discussion: No organization could function if there were one-way communication only. Actually, the required reports are a form of communication to upper management. Management needs these reports to know the results of its earlier orders.

The communication pattern described is typical of an authoritarian or traditionally-structured organization. The "boss" gives orders; the "workers" carry them out and report the results.

In a more democratic or participative organization, employees give themselves specific orders, within the framework of organizational objectives as set out by management. There is no need for constant day-to-day direction from upper managers; employees give themselves the relevant directives. The number of required reports is much less, also.

When workers in a democratic organization communicate with their managers, it is for help in solving problems that they cannot solve by themselves. Since managers do not need to give so many daily orders, they have time to help employees. As a result, a communication pattern develops which is more like that desired by workers: they *can* get through to upper management with their problems and receive help in return; they are given fewer specific orders and are required to submit fewer reports.

With participative management, some of the functions of traditional (authoritarian) management are assumed by employees lower in the organization. Workers are largely self-managing, managers help as well as direct, and the organization is more cooperative and participative at all levels.

3. "Our engineers and project managers spend a lot of time out of the office. They complain that their telephone messages are often mishandled. We also have trouble because telephone orders from customers are frequently miscopied or misunderstood.

How can we make sure telephone messages are complete, accurate and delivered without fail?"
What is your answer?

Discussion: Some problems call for one-time solutions. Others call for policy decisions and implementation of new rules or systems.

The questions above call for policy decisions and a new system, because these are recurring problems.

Errors in telephone order-taking can be reduced by developing a standard telephone order form. This consists of a series of blanks to be filled in by the telephone receptionist. Once the proper questions are listed in proper order, with spaces provided for answers, the only training needed is to teach operators to ask the questions and fill in the blanks. The form itself guarantees that all necessary information is received.

Writing information down ensures that it will not be forgotten. Duplicate copies of forms can be used to ensure that messages will not be lost, even if the original is misplaced. Reading a completed form back to the customer will remove errors of mis-hearing or misinterpretation.

Standard telephone message forms can be used in a similar fashion. In addition, there should be a system for the certain delivery of messages, including places where they will be noticed by the intended party.

Numerous methods for improving communications have been developed by consultants. You may find their personal advice or their books and articles worthwhile. You can solve many communications problems yourself if you learn to recognize when there is a problem, find out what is causing it, and develop your own system for handling it.

CHAPTER 12

UNDERSTANDING WHAT OTHERS MEAN

Understanding messages from others is the other side of the communication process. You will maximize your understanding if you do those things you wish others would do when you are sending them messages.

General Skills of Comprehension

The more thinking you do, and the better your thinking, the more likely you are to understand. Therefore, *ask yourself questions about the message being received*. Ask, "Do I recognize these ideas? How do they fit with my knowledge or experience? What do they mean to me? What do they mean to him or her?"

Listening

"Active Listening" includes
1. Paying Attention.

Direct your attention to the speaker. Watch him. Concentrate on listening and watching without distraction.
2. Encouraging the Speaker.

Make it clear that you want to pay attention to him; show interest; have a pleasant expression.

Ask pertinent questions at appropriate times. Restate what you think he said and ask if you understood correctly.

Do not criticize him or his ideas, do not argue, and do not challenge what he says, even if you disagree with him.
3. Asking Yourself Questions About the Message.

Some useful questions to ask are, "Have I ever experienced anything like that? What is an example? How does this relate to the rest of his message? How important is this point? What evidence has he presented? What evidence might be presented? Why does he believe this? What are his feelings on the matter? What are his motives for telling me about it at this time?"

These and similar questions are important for gaining understanding. The following question is most important of all: *"What does he or she want me to do?"* For example, "Does he want me to sympathize with him, admire him, help him, admit that he is superior to me, excuse him for his failures, or what?"

The "real," underlying meaning of the communication can usually be found once you know what he wants you to do about it.

4. Checking Your Understanding.

Ask her direct questions. Ask for examples. State what you think she meant in your own words, then ask if this is correct. See what she does and compare her words with her actions. This will help you interpret what she said. Also, compare what she says about this topic with her ideas on other subjects.

Reading

"Active Reading" follows the same general principles. One method which has proved very effective is known as "SQRRR." The "S" means, *Survey* the material to be read first. Look over the major headings and summaries. "Q" means, *Question* the material as you read; see if you can find the answers in the text. "R" means, *Read* actively and as quickly as you can without becoming confused or fatigued. The next "R" means, *Recite* to yourself what you have just read. Recite at frequent intervals to find out if you truly understood the material and can now remember it. The last "R" means, *Review* all of the material after you have finished. This puts each part in perspective.

Understanding Non-verbal Messages

Much can be learned about people from the things they do not say but express or reveal in other ways.

For example, people deliberately choose their clothing, hair styles, automobiles, houses, furniture, and many other items in order to convey a desired message about themselves. Expensive clothes, cars, houses and offices say to others, "I am successful; I am important; I expect you to treat me accordingly." Even furniture arrangement can tell you something about the person. A large "executive" desk is commonly used to signify authority or status.

Another form of non-verbal communication is body posture and facial expression. Study of what has been called "body language" reveals a large number of fairly reliable indicators. A person standing with hands on hips is usually impatient, ready to go into action. A person who leans back and crosses his arms across his chest is frequently rejecting what you have to say. One who turns his or her body toward you is usually indicating an acceptance of you into the conversation. (Note: These actions are often unconscious or unintentional. They still serve to reveal the state of feeling which caused them.)

To learn more about body position, facial expression, personal possessions and other non-verbal signals, read some of the many books and articles on the subject. To understand specific signals relevant to your line of work, make yourself aware of people's behavior, observe carefully, and study other managers who are effective in working with people. (This last method is used in training professionals. New psychologists learn to better understand patients by observing experienced practitioners at work.)

SUMMARY

"Active Listening" and "Active Reading" help you pay attention to, think about, and understand messages from others. An important part of this is the asking and answering of questions, such as, "What does this person want me to do?" Always check your understanding by asking more questions and by observing. Study non-verbal signals to develop understanding of that large part of human communication which is not expressed in words.

APPLICATIONS

1. Grade yourself on these understanding skills:
   - Actively paying attention to the other person; encouraging him to communicate with you.
   - Actively thinking about messages being received.
   - Asking questions to promote your understanding, such as

     "What do these words mean to me? What do the words mean to him? What motives and attitudes is he expressing? Why is he telling me these things?
     What does he want me to do?"
   - Concentrating on understanding what the person means, rather than worrying whether his use of words is "correct" or the same as yours.
   - Keeping an open mind when trying to understand; not trying to decide if the message is correct before you are sure you understand it.
   - Having the patience to properly listen, read and think; understanding the other person before you formulate your own response.
   - Wanting to understand others as part of wanting to help them, as well as yourself.

   Practice to improve your skills in these areas. Do the right things, avoid mistakes, and keep at it.

2. What non-verbal or symbolic messages are important in your organization? Which of the following commonly-used symbols of power and position are used there?
   - Size and location of office.
   - Size and location of desk.
   - Normal place of seating at a management meeting (near the boss or the head of the table; beside or across from another department head; at the foot of

the table).

- Clothing worn, including customary or required articles of dress, uniforms, and allowance for personal taste.
- Type of car provided or usually owned; parking place.
- Secretarial help; number of assistants.
- Whether invited to lunch with the boss or executive group.
- Whether invited to social events.
- Personal items, such as size and location of home, types of vacations, ownership of boats or summer houses.
- Contacts outside the corporation, including memberships in civic and charitable organizations on behalf of the company.
- Special privileges allowed.

All managers need to be aware of these and the other non-verbal symbols. They can have great significance. Learn the ones used in your company and profession.

You should make it clear to everyone when a customary non-verbal signal is *not* being used to convey its usual meaning. For instance, if you normally sit beside the boss at meetings, your failure to do so might be taken to mean that you were no longer in the boss's favor. To prevent this misinterpretation, tell people the real reason for your sitting elsewhere, such as having to leave early, wanting to confer with another manager, or not intending to participate in the discussion on this occasion.

Also, be aware of symbolic meanings which may be attached to objects or actions. If the senior typist in the typing pool retires, it might not be a good idea to put the new hiree at his position: the desk itself may have acquired symbolic value as the "head desk" because it was used by the senior person.

EXAMPLES

1. "My parents do not understand me at all! I am a Junior in high school, but they think I am still a little kid who has to be watched all the time. Around our school, if you don't have a car and get to stay out late, then you are socially 'out of it.' How can I make my parents understand?"
What is your answer?

Discussion: Although this sounds like a communication problem, it really is not. Here is a test for communication problems: Would perfect communication solve the problem? In this case, it would not. Failure to "understand" (comprehend) is not the cause of the parents' actions; rather, *they do not agree* with what the teenager wants to do.

Gaining agreement is not the same as gaining understanding. This teenager should try to *convince* her parents that she should be allowed to stay out late, *persuade* them to let her use the car, and *win their confidence* in her ability to avoid trouble.

2. "Fred, one of the older men on the dock, came into my office late Friday afternoon and said that the crew could not get the last shipment out before quitting time. The plant manager told me it had to be done today, so I told Fred that they had to do it before leaving, like it or not. Fred got so angry he cussed me out. Then he and the rest

of them went home anyway. Now, the plant manager is mad at me for not getting the shipment off on time and the men won't talk to me.

What did I do wrong? What could I have done to prevent this mess?"
What is your answer?

Discussion: What the supervisor did wrong was (1) not listening to Fred until he really understood the significance of what he was saying, (2) not showing a desire to help Fred and the men as well as himself and the management, (3) acting in a way that caused anger, resentment and resistance in Fred and the others, and (4) failing to act like a Leader instead of a Boss. What he could have done would have gone something like this:

FRED: "We can't get this shipment out today.

SUPERVISOR: Oh, Fred, what seems to be the problem?

FRED: Here it is, four o'clock on a Friday afternoon, and they send down a last-minute order. This will take at least an extra hour. We are all tired and we want to go home.

SUPERVISOR: I think I know what you mean, but can you tell me some more about it?

FRED: They are always doing this to us. We worked overtime every day this week. Just once, we wanted to get out of here on time.

SUPERVISOR: Yes, there has been a lot of overtime, and I understand how you all feel about it. What would you like me to do?

FRED: I realize it's not your fault, Jim, but we wanted

you to know that we are fed up. We want you to talk to the plant manager about it. We don't want to go through this every Friday.

SUPERVISOR: I understand what you are saying, Fred. I will bring it up with the plant manager at our meeting on Monday. For now, do you think you will be able to get everybody to pull together today to do this last shipment?

FRED: I will tell them what you said. I imagine they will go along this time, but we got'ta get those guys to quit sending down these last minute orders.

SUPERVISOR: Thank you for coming in and talking to me about this. I really appreciate everyone's help. I promise to speak to the plant manager about it Monday and we'll see if we can find a way to improve the situation in the future.

FRED: O.K. Thanks, Jim."

CHAPTER 13

AROUSING
PEOPLE'S INTEREST

Interest: Its Nature and Causes

Interest is that positive feeling or attitude which impels our thought and action toward an objective. Interest is caused by a belief, namely, "Here is something I want or value," or "Here is a way to get something I want." We also feel interest in anything new or unexpected, because we generally like novelty and want to learn about new things.

The causal conditions for interest are *having wants* and *seeing ways to satisfy them*. Therefore, the conditions necessary for you to arouse a person's interest are that he has

- one or more wants which you can help to satisfy;

- confidence that you are willing and able to help him;
- belief that the opportunity exists for the achievement of something he wants;
- belief that he can succeed, and that the rewards will be worth the effort.

Two factors that determine strength of interest are *strength of the underlying want* and *certainty of the belief* that this is a way to satisfy it.

Wants and interests can conflict with each other. Short-term and long-term goals often conflict. You may experience a strong immediate desire for something which is inconsistent with one of your long-range objectives, for example, the immediate pleasure of smoking and the long-range goal of good health. Such conflicts are extremely common.

Here are some other examples:

- Spending money for a good time vs. saving for something wanted later;
- Working on a lengthy project which will be a significant achievement vs. relaxing or working on easier tasks;
- Doing something which will give present gratification but may harm another person vs. maintaining a valuable on-going relationship (cheating on your spouse vs. staying happily married; saying something because you are angry or upset vs. keeping a friend);
- Making a "quick killing" and then having to leave town vs. the slow and steady building of a sound business.

There may also be conflicts between "selfish interests" and other interests. A totally selfish interest would be one that benefitted the individual only. A totally unselfish interest would be one that benefitted others only. However, we cannot feel any interest in a project that does not lead to *something* we want, for some reason. Therefore, a *totally* unselfish interest may be impossible. Even when we desire only to help others, we are still seeking something we want (helping others) and will therefore benefit to some extent when our wants are fulfilled.

This is not to say that it is impossible to be truly altruistic. We *can* want something solely because it will benefit another person. We can want something for others, even at the expense of our more-selfish interests. This possibility is demonstrated by the obvious fact that many people do desire to help others, and by the heroic actions of those who have sacrificed much – even their lives – to help another.

Which strategy do you think is best: the pursuit of short-term goals or long-range interests? This is a serious issue for every individual and organization. The question has no easy answer in real life. On the one hand, exclusive pursuit of short-term goals may mean that long-range objectives cannot be met. There are some old folk sayings to illustrate the folly of this strategy, including, "A stitch in time saves nine," and "Take care of your pennies and the dollars will take care of themselves." On the other hand, exclusive pursuit of long-term goals can be equally disastrous, as illustrated by, "Eat, drink and be merry for tomorrow we die," and "Stop and smell the roses along the way."

Obviously, we must achieve a balance. It is up to you to discover that balance in your job, in your organization or department, and for your life as a whole. One illustration of a balance between "selfish" and "unselfish" interests is contained in our concept of Leadership: we do best when we look for those projects which will benefit ourselves *and other people at the same time.*

Mistakes to Avoid

1. Failure to think about the other person's wants, instead of exclusively our own, is the principal cause of failure to arouse interest. We must think about the other individual's desires and how to help him satisfy them. We must overcome the natural tendency for our own wants to dominate all our thinking.

2. Another mistake is trying to force a person to "take an interest." This does not work. We cannot say that she "should be interested," either. If the conditions for interest are not present, the person *cannot* be interested.

3. We must not assume that our interest in a topic will be contagious. Others are interested in topics of value to them, but not necessarily in topics of value to us.

4. There will always be resistance to any effort to arouse interest. People want to satisfy their present wants, but they do not necessarily want us arousing new wants in them. Also, new interests would require them to change, which will meet the usual human reluctance to making any changes which can be avoided.

Therefore, expect resistance whenever interest must be aroused.

Other causes of resistance to arousing interest are that
- the person may be well satisfied with things as they are;
- she may have a conflict of interests (wants) which are interfering;
- she may be interested in the project but is resisting because she does not like *your* actions or attitude

(Are you being too domineering, self-centered or manipulative?);

- she may have to change too many cherished beliefs and established positions to accept your suggestion; she may decide that the rewards would not be worth what she would have to give up.

5. We may bore people. Interest in a presentation must be stimulated by relating it to the wants of the audience. Attention and curiosity must be maintained through novel material and presentation methods. The pace must be fast enough to maintain interest but not so fast as to confuse.

6. We must remember that interest will fade over time. It can be lost completely if any of the necessary conditions are removed. For example, if the want which initially sparked interest is satisfied or no longer exists, then interest based upon that want must vanish. A person will lose interest if she does not receive the expected benefits after a reasonable period of time. She will then lose faith in the project. Or, she may be disappointed in the quality of the benefits received, in the amount they are costing her, or in the rewards received compared to those available elsewhere. Finally, she may come to assume that the rewards will continue without sustained effort on her part.

How To Arouse and Sustain Interest

1. To arouse interest, start by making a plan of action. Be certain of your purposes: Do you sincerely want to help this person get something he wants? List the benefits to be gained from *his* point of view. Plan how you will guide his thinking toward the conclusion that this is a good way to achieve what he wants. Use questions, suggestions and illustrations, as well as statements.

Expect resistance. Prepare yourself to handle it calmly. Do not take it personally.

Then, follow these steps:

- Make the person consciously aware of (be thinking about) his unsatisfied wants. Employ questions, stories or other methods to focus his attention on these relevant wants. If possible, get the person to *say* that he is dissatisfied and wants to find a way to achieve his goals. Better yet, have the person ask you if you know a way for him to solve his problem.
- Show him a way to satisfy his want. Convince him that your suggestion would solve his problem. Provide evidence.
- Show him that the proposed action would be effective, would be worth the cost, and would be better than doing anything else.
- At this point, his interest should be aroused. Further steps would involve convincing and persuading, which are discussed in the next two chapters.

If you wish to arouse interest in a topic or presentation, relate what you have to say to the wants and interests of the audience. For example, describe a problem which you know they are now facing, then present a possible solution.

Learn to use novelty, unexpected facts, dramatic illustrations and information that contradicts what your listeners previously believed. Arouse their curiosity by keeping them wondering what is coming next.

Utilize the two general priorities of human interest: people are most interested in themselves and things that directly affect them, and secondly, in learning about other people.

2. To sustain or regain interest, recreate those conditions that first aroused interest. Keep people aware of the rewards they are receiving or will receive. Remind them that the benefits will not be forthcoming without their continuing effort. Show ways that the present rewards might be increased. Show how this enterprise could lead on to greater things. Keep up a feeling of movement and progress.

Have people convince others about the project. As we convince others, we tend to convince ourselves.

If interest has died out completely, find out why it was lost. Then, see if the original want is still present. If it is, re-convince the people that the plan can work. Remind them of the efforts that they have already devoted to its success. Provide or point out additional benefits. Ask them to rejoin the effort.

When you lose the interest of an audience, immediately try something different. Stage a dramatic incident, show movies or pictures, tell a story, evoke vivid mental images, get the audience involved by asking for their comments and questions, start a discussion, ask for examples, stage an application exercise such as a case study or role-play, sing a song, take a break – anything that makes it interesting again!

3. Eventually, you will come to the end of what you have to say that is new and is related to their wants. When you do, quit!

SUMMARY

Interest is a feeling that follows from the discovery of something of value or a way to achieve something wanted. We arouse interest when we relate new information in a novel, attention-getting way, and when we show people how they can achieve one or more of their goals. Interest is strongest when the person is consciously aware of his unsatisfied wants, believes strongly in our plan, and has confidence in everyone who will be involved.

APPLICATIONS

Arousing interest has four major areas of application for managers. The first is arousing workers' interest in doing their work well and in achieving sufficient productivity. Another is arousing the interest of superiors or peers in an idea or project. The third is arousing the interest of customers in the product or services provided. The fourth is arousing the interest of investors, creditors, government regulators or others in some matter of importance.

For instance, to gain the interest of upper management in a project you wish to initiate, show them how it will help *them* meet some of *their* goals. Research their priorities ahead of time so you can phrase your proposal appropriately.

This skill can also be used for arousing your own interest or reviving it when it begins to fade. For example, to re-arouse your interest in work when you start to "go stale," set definite goals and formulate plans for their achievement. You might also change your routine: enroll in advanced training, try new methods of production, or make adjustments in your personal life.

You will find additional applications for these skills outside the job. The interest of children in school work can be enhanced the same way you create job interest among employees.

Consider the following typical parental complaint: "My children are not interested in school, in studying, or in doing their homework. All they want to do is watch T.V., run around with their friends, play sports, and spend my money. What can I do?"

If you have children, you know how difficult this situation can be. Ultimately, of course, you will have to work out your own solution, adjusted to you, them and the particular circumstances.

Here are some methods that have worked for other parents:

- Parental attention and help;
- Field trips and direct experiences with study objects;
- Individual projects;
- Making rewards, such as getting to go out or participate in sports, dependent upon success in academic courses;
- Payment or other rewards for good grades;
- Having wholesome companions and activities;
- Encouragement of significant long-range goals which will require present and future education;
- Setting a good example of continuing learning by parents.

EXAMPLES

1. "As plant manager for a semi-automated electronics company, I see all the problems routine work can cause. We have missing parts, skipped assembly steps, sloppy soldering, poor finishing and damage from careless handling. The jobs here are boring, without a doubt, but someone has to do them. How can we get our people to take an interest in the work and in doing a good job?"

What is your answer?

Discussion: Unfortunately, no one can *make* a person interested in a job when all the conditions needed to make it interesting are missing. Some changes will be necessary.

One method for increasing job interest is called "Job Rotation," where workers alternate between different jobs. This keeps each person interested by varying the routine, but does not change the nature of the work itself.

Another method is "Job Enrichment," in which the task itself is made more complex and challenging. Instead of always soldering the same circuit board in the same four places, a production employee might assemble the entire instrument, test it, and pack it for shipment.

A further step is an application of "Management By Objectives," where assembly-level personnel design and implement the production methods. Top management sets the objectives; floor management and workers formulate plans, carry out the operations, and supervise their own work.

Other ways to make jobs more interesting include
- social interactions (having people work in teams),
- production contests,
- incentives of various kinds (even boring jobs can be done well if the right incentives are provided),
- improvement in physical working conditions.

Finally, a solution may be found in better selection of personnel. Some people do not mind repetitious work. In some cases, developmentally disabled workers have been both productive and satisfied in jobs that other people found too limiting.

Ultimately, any totally repetitious job might be best handled through automation. A machine can be faster, more reliable and cheaper than a human being, and it does not become bored.

2. "I got stuck with organizing the annual company picnic. These things have been so dull in the past that no one wants to come, let alone help. How can I get people interested in helping out and making it a success? It will look terrible in front of the boss if the picnic 'bombs' again!"
What is your answer?

Discussion: No one is going to be interested in anything called "The Annual Company Picnic" if it has always been a disaster. The first thing to do is change its name and image. Begin by finding out what employees and management would like to do at a picnic or outing. Plan the activities around these wants. Publicize the event in such a way that the desired features are emphasized.

Find out what other organizations have done that were successful. Select ideas which have the greatest potential for your event.

Get others involved in planning and running the picnic. People are naturally more interested if they have a part, and they are less likely to criticize if they are involved.

3. "A young man in my department is not performing his work satisfactorily. Six months ago he started as our 'stock boy,' an entry-level position. It was his first job

after graduation from high school. Now, he shows little interest in the job, in doing it right or in helping others. I still think he has a lot of potential. There must be something about the position itself which is bothering him. How can I get him to see that taking an interest in his work and doing a good job are necessary if he is to advance?"

What is your answer?

Discussion: You have now read most of this book, so you should be able to formulate a plan for handling this kind of problem. Write out your analysis of the situation, including probable causes for this employee's attitude and possible steps the supervisor could take to correct the problem.

Some questions to consider:

- How would the supervisor *find out* what is causing his lack of interest?
- How can the supervisor *keep* from arousing his resentment and resistance when his work is criticized?
- What should the supervisor say *if he cannot* provide the kind of benefits the employee wants?
- What should the supervisor do *if he is unable* to arouse his interest in doing a better job?

CHAPTER 14

CONVINCING OTHERS THAT WHAT YOU SAY IS CORRECT

What is Convincing?

Convincing is
- causing a person to have a belief;
- gaining acceptance of what you say;
- reaching agreement among a group of people;
- changing beliefs and attitudes.

Convincing always involves changing beliefs. If they already believed what you said, there would be no need to convince them.

People naturally resist changing their beliefs. How many of your present beliefs do you think are false? None, of course, or you would not hold those beliefs.

Therefore, if someone wanted to change one of your beliefs, you would tend to resist. The same applies to others.

Because all belief is based on a person's thinking, changing belief can only be accomplished by causing the person to do some new thinking. When you convince, you lead the person to think about the matter again, perhaps using new information, a different viewpoint, or better logic. You guide him toward the conclusions you want, but you must let him do his own thinking.

Since there will always be some resistance to changing a belief, you should practice those methods which lessen resistance. Do not argue; do not make the person "back down" or lose face; keep the discussion friendly; sustain a good relationship and a good mood during the discussion.

Difficulty will be encountered whenever causal conditions favoring argument are present. Other conditions which can arouse resistance are emotionally-charged topics – which are often difficult to predict – and the person's attitude toward you. If they dislike you, some people will argue with any statements you make, even ones they actually accept. Likewise, they will agree with almost anything said by someone they like or admire.

What Causes Failure To Convince?

Mistakes made while trying to win agreement include the following:

1. Doing any of the things which cause arguments.

Arguing is the single biggest mistake anyone can make in trying to convince. People make this obvious mistake time and time again, because they do not know any better. They do not know an effective method for convincing, so they use the only method they do know (argument). Not only is this method ineffective, it actually makes the situation worse by arousing more resistance from the listener.

2. Going beyond the other person's experience or capacity to reason on the topic.

No one can be convinced about anything on which he is incapable of thinking. No one is capable of thinking about topics completely beyond his experience. His ability to think is also limited by his innate abilities, his training and his learned reasoning skills.

Sometimes, people will decide to believe what you say even though they cannot reason it out for themselves. This is possible because they use their experience with *you*, plus their experience with other people, to reach the conclusion, "I can believe it because this person says it is true, even though I do not understand the reasons." Strictly speaking, such reasoning is never logically justifiable. However, as a practical matter, it is done often and done successfully in everyday life. To make it work for you, you must first win people's confidence that you form your opinions on good evidence. You must be seen as an individual with good judgment, whose word can be accepted with assurance.

3. Using threat or force.

A person cannot be convinced through force or threat. A threatened person may *say* he believes, but only to escape the consequences of vocal disagreement. Inside, such a person is thinking, "I will tell him I agree, but I really do not." There is an old folk saying which summarizes this point: "A man convinced against his will is of the same opinion still."

Agreements made under threat will be withdrawn or

ignored later, just as contracts made under coercion are held to be legally void.

If we are unable to convince people in a situation which requires an immediate decision, then we may have to force compliance. An example is dealing with children who are too young for effective thinking on the subject. Another example: employees who are new on the job or are inexperienced in the particular problems involved.

If we do use force in situations like these, we can hope that later developments will convince everyone that we were correct in our opinions and were right to go ahead.
4. Trying too hard to convince.

Giving the impression that you want very much to convince a person may make him suspicious. People will doubt what you say if they think you *want to believe* these things or *will benefit from convincing them*. On the other hand, they will usually believe if they know you to be a person who forms beliefs *only* on the basis of good evidence and sound reasoning.

When you seem overly anxious to convince, people wonder if you are anxious because you are not sure yourself or because you may receive some significant reward at their expense. Doubts like these will make it difficult for them to believe anything you say.

How Can Convincing Skill Be Developed?

1. Planning and practice are the keys to developing any skill.

Plan in detail for important convincing tasks, such as presenting a major proposal to the executive committee. Study the situation, the topic, the people, and the ideas you want to put across. Plan how you will conduct yourself, how you will handle the expected resistance to your proposals, how you will guide their thinking based upon their beliefs, and how you will create and maintain a pleasant, cooperative atmosphere.

Then, do a "Mental Rehearsal" of your performance. To use this technique, imagine yourself acting and feeling the way you want it to happen during the actual meeting. Picture it as vividly as you can. See yourself doing exactly what you planned.

For very important presentations, you may want to stage a real rehearsal as well as the mental one. Speak out loud. Record what you say. Have others listen and react. Use this information to improve your planning and your performance.

Beware of memorizing particular words or phrases. A memorized speech often sounds insincere. Do not become a slave to the presentation exactly as you have planned it. Remain flexible, so you can succeed even if reactions are not what you foresaw.

2. The secret of convincing is this:
    - *Emphasize* those points upon which you and the other people *agree*; use these to lead their thinking to the desired conclusion;
    - *De-emphasize* points upon which you and the other people *disagree*; ignore these, they can only lead to argument.

    Agreement is always built on agreement.

    To emphasize points of agreement:
    - Search for beliefs upon which all agree or can agree;
    - Ask questions and listen carefully to learn what others accept; look for beliefs that coincide with yours;
    - Use shared convictions as starting points for a line of thought; lead others to new thinking by using the beliefs they already have.

To de-emphasize points of disagreement:

- Find out people's opinions on the matter ahead of the discussion; use questions to explore readiness for a new idea; refrain from stating opinions you know others will not accept;
- Make few blunt assertions of your opinion; instead, use suggestions, questions and indirect ways of presenting concepts; lead others to think about the subject with an open mind; offer thoughts to consider, instead of conclusions already drawn;
- When you offer evidence, do not claim that it settles the issue; let them decide if it does (When you claim that the evidence is conclusive, you seem to say that they have to accept your conclusion whether they want to or not.);
- Admit your mistakes, if there are any; this encourages others to admit that they may have been wrong on some issues; it creates an atmosphere in which they can alter their former beliefs without becoming embarrassed or appearing to have lost a debate with you;
- Keep an atmosphere of "me against you" from developing (two sides in opposition); do not think of others as opponents; do not try to "win," even in your own mind; do not become upset if you are not able to convince them immediately; keep an open mind, as you want them to do. (Remember: it is *possible* that they are right and you are wrong on this issue.)

If disagreement does emerge:

- Do not argue;
- Retrace the conversation until you find where the difference of opinion emerged (where you still had

agreement and were thinking together toward the next step);

- If you can, clear up the disagreement by removing any misunderstandings of each other's positions; use the methods of Making Yourself Clearly Understood and Understanding What Others Mean; convince by reasoning from opinions they already hold;
- Then, move ahead again, toward the desired conclusion.

If disagreement cannot be removed by this method, find another line of reasoning. Do not keep arguing about matters upon which you disagree.

3. Avoid "trying too hard."

- Stay "cool." We all have a tendency to overestimate the importance of our immediate concerns. Counteract over-anxiety by attaining a broader perspective. Ask yourself, "Will this really make or break me? Will success or failure determine the course of the rest of my life? Or, is this just one more momentary crisis, neither more nor less important than a thousand others?" Usually, you will find that it was not as great a problem as you initially thought.
- Keep your own importance in perspective. We all tend to think of ourselves as the center of the universe, but other people are concerned primarily with themselves. Even a life-and-death matter for you may be seen as "not very important" by others.
- Concentrate on the person to whom you are speaking; exclude from your immediate consciousness all thoughts about yourself and what you want. By thinking about the other person, you greatly in-

crease your chances for appreciating his point of view and guiding his thought to the desired conclusion.

SUMMARY

Convincing is the opposite of argument. In argument, we concentrate on points of disagreement; in convincing, we start with points of agreement and think together step-by-step to the desired conclusion. To convince, start with the beliefs people already hold and lead their thinking forward; avoid threat and force; do not "try too hard."

APPLICATIONS

Select a real situation in which you will have to convince someone. Plan how you will do it. Include an analysis of the people involved, their present points of view (opinions), which beliefs will have to be changed, exactly what you want to achieve, problems which are likely to arise, possible starting points (common beliefs), the best time and place, preliminary steps to take, the presentation plan, the personal impression to be made, how you will handle resistance, and how you will handle failure if necessary.

EXAMPLES

1. "I am sales manager for a furniture manufacturer. The owner likes a certain style of furniture, for which the company has been famous over fifty years. The problem is that this style is no longer popular. Nobody wants it! The boss will still not change our lines because of company tradition and his own personal preferences. I have shown him market studies and preference polls, but he

rejects them all.

How can I get him to see that his favorite style is now hopelessly out of date? How can I get him to accept the data on present consumer preferences? How can I get him to change his mind when he does not want to change?"
What is your answer?

Discussion: A person holding a set opinion can find some reason for rejecting *any* and *all* evidence which conflicts with his desired conclusion. No matter what data the sales manager presents, the boss could find a way to disqualify it.

One solution is to put the boss in a position where he would have to accept the truth. Obtain agreement in advance on the method to be used for determining what people now prefer in furniture styles. If the boss rejects the surveys of furniture store shoppers, get him to say what kind of survey or other evidence he will accept. Once a mutually-acceptable method is adopted, it is a simple matter of carrying out the method and seeing the results, which he would have to accept.

We use a similar method for settling political disagreements in a democracy. We may disagree on who should be president, for example, but we agree on a *method for deciding*, namely, an election. Whoever wins the election, we have agreed in advance, should hold the office.

These examples illustrate one method for gaining agreement: *decide on a method for deciding.* Use the method and let the results speak for themselves.

2. "My friend and co-worker has just brought me a petition to sign. It accuses our supervisor of being unfair to Jimmy Smith by giving him an unjustified and highly-negative performance evaluation.

I do not doubt that the evaluation was unfair. The supervisor has it in for Jimmy. However, I do not like the idea of a petition. I think management will take it as a challenge. They will say this is none of our business and side with the supervisor. They may even find ways to get back at those who signed it.

My uncle is one of the plant managers. I think he would help if I explained the situation to him.

How can I get my friend to drop the petition and let me see if I can solve the problem without creating a confrontation with management?"

What is your answer?

Discussion: Convincing the co-worker to drop the petition will be difficult because the petition is the co-worker's idea. No one likes to drop an idea he created, especially when he has taken a public stand on it.

If these two disagree on a method for helping Jimmy Smith, upon what do they agree? They agree on the fact that Jimmy got an unfair report and they agree on the objective of helping Jimmy by overturning that report. If this worker can get his friend to expand his concept of the objective to include "helping Jimmy by overturning the unfair evaluation *and* staying out of trouble ourselves in doing so," then he could, possibly, get his friend to re-evaluate the alternatives.

He could acknowledge that the petition was one possible way to proceed. He would then ask what other possibilities there were. He would try to get his friend to consider these. If he was successful, they would list the alternatives, including a private conversation with the uncle. He would have to convince his friend that the private conversation would be the best choice because it is most likely to lead to a solution without getting them all into unnecessary trouble. The petition could be kept as an alternative to be used if all else failed.

This example illustrates another method for gaining agreement: agree on the primary *goal* to be achieved; then expand the statement of that goal to include *all objectives* to be attained, not just the primary one. Consider all the alternatives; then pick the best, the second best, and so on, to be tried in that order.

CHAPTER 15

PERSUADING PEOPLE TO TAKE ACTION

When the movie gangster says, "We'll send the boys around to 'persuade' you to pay," real persuasion is *not* what he has in mind.

What is persuasion? It is causing an action or a decision to act through the use of reason, that is, by leading a person to think.

Persuading takes a step beyond convincing. Whereas convincing ends in belief, persuasion ends in action. When we persuade, we use all the skills covered so far.

Why Persuasion Is Better Than Its Alternatives

In persuading, we cause a person to see that the action we recommend is the best thing he can do for his own benefit, under the circumstances.

There are alternative methods for causing action, although none is as effective overall as persuasion. They include the following:

1. Force or threat.

The first problem with force is that people resist it. The effort we must expend to force someone to act is often more than the result is worth. The second problem is revenge, which people seek if we are successful in forcing them. We can put ourselves in deep trouble with this method.

2. Begging.

Begging is unreliable because people often refuse it. It is also unpleasant and demeaning.

3. Inspiration.

Inspiration causes action through positive emotion. People admire an inspirational leader and follow the example set. When inspiration works, it is a wonderful method. Unfortunately, it is insufficiently reliable for most managers who are not highly-charismatic. Even when they set a good example, employees may fail to imitate the behavior.

4. Arousing strong emotion.

Some managers lead by deliberate emotional arousal. They try to get their people "fired up." They stage pep rallies and have motivational speakers, contests, group activities and meetings. Others seek to create a team spirit, promote ambition and competitiveness, provide social rewards of acceptance and punishments of rejection. They encourage pride in receiving group recognition.

A major problem with these methods is that emotions are by their nature temporary. They must be constantly re-aroused. Also, methods of emotional arousal become less effective over time. Therefore, it requires great expenditure of time and effort to constantly motivate people in this way.

Another problem is that strong emotion can get out of control. It may lead to unwanted consequences, such as cheating to achieve results, high stress levels and eventual "job burn out."

5. Going it alone.

Sometimes managers are tempted to forget about trying to arouse others to action because it is just too much trouble. Instead, they try to do everything themselves or everything they cannot get their employees to do. The problem with this is that managers are hired to manage the work of others. If they are doing the work themselves, then they are not managing. If managers are not managing, then no one is.

Each of these strategies *would* be appropriate in some circumstances. However, for most managers, most of the time, they are not as effective as persuasion.

When Persuasion Is Impossible

Persuasion can occur only if the necessary causal conditions are present. Because we rely on leading the other person to think, all conditions for thinking must be present. The person must want to think about the subject; he must see a way to obtain something he wants. He must have enough confidence in us to listen to us. We must gain his favorable attention, and convince him that what we say is true. Conditions which may cause resistance or resentment must be avoided.

Other conditions unfavorable to persuading would include

- a poor attitude on your part, perhaps because you

think persuasion is too much trouble, or you would rather use authority;
- a negative opinion of you, on his part;
- your inability to persuade;
- distractions caused by other pressing matters;
- assumptions on the part of either of you that persuasion is not necessary or would not be effective here.

In some circumstances, persuasion *is* impractical, if not totally impossible. These would include
- dealing with young children, or adults who are unable to think effectively about the matter at hand;
- emergency conditions, when there is no time for thinking or persuading; (Note that emergency agencies persuade their personnel in advance that it is important to follow orders without question when emergency conditions are in effect.);
- an irresolvable conflict of purposes or interests among the people involved.

How To Persuade

Successful persuasion makes use of all the leadership skills. Review earlier chapters first when planning an important persuasion exercise.

There are four stages to persuasion, with several steps in each.

1. The Preliminary Stage

First, attract favorable attention to yourself and to the matter you wish to discuss. Capture and recapture attention through action and dramatic incidents. Put the most important points in positions of emphasis.

Second, gain people's confidence by giving evidence of your competence and desire to help them.

Demonstrate your ability, sincerity, knowledge, integrity and any other characteristic needed.

Third, arouse their interest in the matter. Create an urge to think by showing how this can lead to something they want.

2. The Reasoning Stage

The heart of persuasion is practical reasoning (decision making). *You* lead the person to do this reasoning. (See the relevant sections in the chapter on productive thinking.)

Remember: As you guide the person's thinking, it is still his thinking. You must allow him to do it. You cannot force a person to become persuaded.

Step #1:

By completing The Preliminary Stage, you have aroused his interest in achieving a goal he desires. At this point, he will think, "I have an unsatisfied want which I wish to satisfy."

Step #2:

He now asks himself, "How can I achieve the objective?" He may ask you this question. If he does, you can proceed without fear of resistance. If he does not ask, you may ask him if he would be interested in a solution.

Step #3:

You now present your proposal, the action you want him to take to get what he wants (and help you get what you want). This is the time to use your communication skills. Be sure he understands your proposal.

Step #4:

He will now evaluate your proposal. Do *not* try to prevent this. Some of the questions he will ask himself are, "Would it really work? What would it cost in time, money, etc.? Could I do it? Would it be worth the cost?"

Step #5:

If your proposal passes these tests, he will then ask himself, "Is this the best alternative?" To answer the question, he must examine other possible courses of action. You cannot prevent him from this consideration. Help him evaluate the alternatives by presenting information on their good and bad features (from his point of view).

Step #6:

Next, convince him that the proposed action is superior to all the alternatives. Remember that doing nothing is always one of his alternatives. He must be convinced that following your plan is better than any of the other possibilities, including those of doing nothing or not deciding at all.

Step #7:

If you are successful, he now concludes, "The plan he proposed is the best thing I could do. I should do it."

So ends The Reasoning Stage of the persuasion process.

3. The Transition Stage

At the end of The Reasoning Stage, these two alternatives are weighed:

- To do the action, pay the costs and receive the benefits;
- To omit the action, save the costs and forfeit the benefits.

In evaluating these alternatives, the person uses his *feeling toward each* as a criterion. This feeling may be called "preferring," "liking," "feeling good about," "feeling certain of," "feeling a desire for," or simply "deciding."

If the proposed action passes the preference/feeling test, then, *he feels like doing it.*

4. The Intensification-of-Feeling Stage

Feeling is the immediate cause of action. To be effective, a feeling must be sufficiently strong to impel action and it must be stronger than any counter-impulses. Therefore, the final stage in the persuasion process is the intensification of the "feeling-like-acting."

When a person completes The Reasoning Stage, he is convinced that he should do what you suggest. (Of course, convincing is never enough. He still may not act because he does not feel like it.) When he completes The Transition Stage, he feels some impulse to act. Your next task is to intensify that impulse until it is strong enough to trigger the desired decision or action.

To do this, you must appeal to his emotions. There are many ways to do so:

- You could emphasize again the attractive features of your proposal. Get him to visualize himself enjoying the benefits.
- Bring up other advantages which you have not mentioned before. Sales people do this frequently. The record companies that advertise on television wait until the end of their commercial to tell you about the "free bonus record" you will receive for ordering right away. They know that this will intensify your desire to accept their offer. If they told you about the bonus record earlier, they would have had nothing to use at the end to "clinch" the deal.
- Tell vivid stories of how others have enjoyed their rewards. Give a demonstration of the product or benefit to be received. Provide a concrete experience if possible.
- Remind him of the cost of not taking the action (missing all those benefits). Appeal to his pride,

position, and intelligence.
- Get him to talk about what he would like to do. Be reluctant to tell him everything. Allow his imagination to work. He may talk himself into the decision. (Whether you tell all or let him imagine for himself will depend upon your evaluation of his personality and the best strategy in this particular case.)

If your efforts have been successful, the person now feels strongly that he wants to do the action. Will he do it? If so, when?

To gain a decision for immediate action, you may have to create a sense of urgency, an urge to do it *now*.

Among the various methods available, the simplest is to just ask him for a decision. To answer your question, he has to make a decision now.

Another method is to suggest that enough time has been spent on the issue, that there is nothing to be gained by additional deliberation. If he suggests a further postponement, point out the costs of delay, such as having this decision hanging over his head even longer, losing the incentives you offered for taking immediate action, and postponing enjoyment of the benefits.

If he asks for "time to think it over," you should offer to wait while he does so. Your presence will create an additional incentive to decide now. If he still delays, set a definite time for a final answer.

Sometimes an issue is truly pressing and calls for action without hesitation. If this is the case, explain the situation and ask for an immediate answer.

Here are some special considerations which apply when persuading a group of people:
- Ask for a meeting of *everyone* who will be in on the decision;

- Put on a good show; use appropriate dramatics and group-presentation techniques;
- Establish your credentials *before* your presentation; credibility is essential before a group;
- Plan thoroughly; rehearse everything you will do;
- Have some of the group members persuaded of your position before the meeting; the more influential they are, the better for you.

SUMMARY

Persuasion is an effective and desirable method for causing action. It uses all the leadership skills, including Attracting Favorable Attention, Winning Confidence, Arousing Interest, Leading People to Think (Practical Reasoning), Communicating, and Convincing. The final step is arousing and intensifying those feelings which will impel the action.

APPLICATIONS

Analyze your own feelings about persuasion. Some feel that they should not have to persuade anybody, especially not subordinates. Others feel that persuasion is not assertive enough. Managers with authoritarian motives dislike it because it counters the reasons they became managers in the first place. Some may fear that employees will regard them as weak if they do not "boss them around."

In some circumstances, persuasion is not practical. Decide when you should use persuasion, and when other methods will serve you better. You will almost always have to use it in dealing with your superiors, customers, and professional peers. These people rarely respond favorably to anything else.

As a practice exercise and to develop your ability, plan in detail how you will persuade a group or individual in a real situation. List the steps of persuasion. Then, write out what you will do to accomplish each step. Plan how you will handle problems, how you will act, what you will say, and how you will react to positive or negative developments at each stage.

EXAMPLES

1. "I am an administrative officer in a traditional organization. Our system is built on authority in both structure and procedure. I don't see how I could use persuasion when the whole organization is based on authority. I would be afraid that my superiors would think I am not doing my job and subordinates would lose respect."
What is your answer?

Discussion: The most ambitious application would be to persuade the top managers to shift the entire organization over to a persuasive management philosophy. This might be difficult, but it could pay off handsomely. The manager should first learn as much as possible about applications of persuasion in management. Then, he would persuade top executives that they had the most to gain by changing to these techniques throughout the company.

An alternative would be the application of persuasion in the manger's department. Explaining the procedure to both upper-management and employees could offset any doubts about the manger's methods.

Another application would involve use of persuasion in only those situations where there is a genuine choice of action. For example, there may be no choice about what must be done, but there could be a choice of methods for meeting those goals. The manager could use non-authoritarian methods in these instances.

Regardless of how authoritarian an organization may be, persuasion is still the only method allowed for certain relationships. A subordinate must use persuasion to change management decisions. A manager must use persuasion in dealing with superiors, customers, regulators, investors, others outside the structure of the organization, and his management peers.

If current personnel cannot be shaken from their authoritarian habits, there is still hope in the next generation. Train younger managers in persuasive techniques. When they reach the higher ranks, they will be skilled in the persuasive method and can implement it throughout the company.

2. "I am president of a professional trade association. The other officers and I do not get along. They are 'old guard'; I was elected because I promised change.

According to our constitution, any major project must have the approval of the management committee, consisting of the officers. I want to make some major changes. I think the members are behind me on these.

How can I get the other officers to agree, when they resist everything I propose?"
What is your answer?

Discussion: If *any* change suggested by the president is likely to be rejected, she may be the last person who should propose a major project. She could have someone else make the proposals. The best kind of person would be (1) another member of the management committee, especially an influential one, (2) a credible outsider, or (3) a member of the organization who represents a significant portion of the membership.

Some possible strategies, in addition to the above, are

• Reverse Psychology.

The president would use "reverse psychology" by seeming to oppose the proposal. If other officers automatically oppose anything she supports, this could swing their vote toward approval of the proposal.

• Presentation of a Problem.

Instead of making a proposal, the president would point out a problem. She would say, "Here is a problem we face as an organization. Are there any suggestions for a solution?" Since the president has not proposed anything, there is no possibility of opposition to her proposal. Then, she would wait for individuals in the committee to suggest a solution. When one of them suggests what the president thinks is the best answer, she, as moderator, could keep directing conversation back to this alternative. She could encourage recognition of the faults in any other plans proposed. At the psychologically-right time, she would ask for approval of the favored plan.

• An Individual Approach.

The president could persuade individual officers before the meeting, by using whatever arguments or offers would be effective in each case. She would have one of these pre-persuaded officers propose the project, then help guide discussion toward approval.

In persuading this resistant group, the president would still follow all the steps of persuasion. She could start by drawing their attention to the problem to be solved. She might win their confidence by displaying an attitude of wanting to help the organization regardless of who got the credit. She could arouse interest in the project by making the committee actively aware of the desires of the membership and possible benefits to them.

She would then guide the group through the stages of practical reasoning: Consciousness of a want, search for a solution, consideration of alternatives, preference for the proposed action and arrival at a "feeling like doing."

The impulse to act could be intensified by additional incentives, fear of losing the benefits, need for the benefits now, need to make a decision now, and group enthusiasm for the idea.

3. The vice president of a medium-sized college learned of a government program to fund foreign-language learning centers. These were buildings which housed all the offices, classrooms, living quarters and dining facilities for language students and faculty. The vice president thought this sounded like a good idea, so he had an architect design a building. He took a model of the new center to a meeting of the college's language department heads.

After the vice president finished explaining his proposal, the department heads sat in silence for several minutes. Then, one of them said, "Mr. Vice President, you have a lot of nerve!" With that, they all walked out. (They did not approve the plan.)

Why?

What is your answer?

Discussion: Having read the book to this point, you should be able to analyze the situation and say why the proposal failed. What did the vice president do wrong? Why were the department heads offended? What should he have done instead, to gain their approval for the project?

4. "I am the new sales manager for a builder of single-family homes. How can I design a sales and marketing plan for these houses?"
What is your answer?

Discussion: Here is an outline for a possible sales and marketing plan.
1. The Preliminary Steps

Attract favorable attention to your product through advertising and model homes. Decorate the houses to be striking, even if the decoration is somewhat overdone. Salesmen can gain favorable attention by their good appearance, competence, and an attitude of helpfulness toward customers.

Win customers' confidence in the company by showing its length of time in business, its successes and its reputation. Confidence in the homes themselves can be developed by providing explanations of building features and by the direct personal experience of showing prospects through the model home.

The attitudes of sales people toward potential customers are extremely important. They should be non-pressuring, confidence-inspiring, and helpful.

Arousing interest is accomplished in large part by the location and features of the homes. When people see these beautiful houses, on attractive lots in nice neighborhoods, they will immediately think about their own housing desires. The sales person can encourage interest by having prospects talk about what they want in a home or what they dislike about their present accommodations. Salesmen should learn as much as possible about the needs and wants of their prospects. For example, do they have six children, does he like gardening, does she want a shopping center nearby?

2. The Reasoning Steps

The prospects now say to themselves, "We want a new home like these. How can we get the house we want?"

They ask the salesman, "What do you have that could satisfy our needs?"

You, the sales person, now show them houses and lots that you think would best satisfy their needs, bearing in mind what they desire and what they can afford.

They evaluate your proposal. If it seems to satisfy their requirements, they will proceed to the next step.

Before deciding to buy, all sensible people would now consider their alternatives. This is especially true for a major purchase, such as a house. Show them how your offering is a better way to satisfy their needs than any of the alternatives.

By this step, you will have convinced the prospects that your house is the best choice for them. They will now conclude, "This is the best choice for us. We should do it."

3. The Transition Stage

Your prospective customers are almost ready to make their decision. They feel a desire for your product because you have convinced them that this is the best thing they can do. As they reconsider the possibilities, they may want to revisit the home you showed them. Allow this, as often as desired. The more time they spend in the house, the more they may feel a desire for it.

It is important to recall that every customer sells himself. You cannot force a person to select your listing; you can only present it in the best way. They will make their own decision, often on the basis of factors you never knew existed.

If you are successful, the prospect will now feel a strong preference for your offering.

4. The Intensification-of-Feeling Stage

Have the family imagine themselves living in the house, engaged in their favorite activities, enjoying its many attractive features. Get them to talk about how they would decorate, remodel, landscape, or use the home. Have them imagine a warm fire in the family-room fireplace when they return from skating on the neighborhood pond, having friends over for dinner, and other positive emotional experiences.

Create an impulse to close the sale by offering a "special bonus" such as lower financing costs, free landscaping, or a quick delivery date. Tell them the reasons for deciding now: interest rates may go up, prices may go up, lots in this subdivision may be sold out. Take them back to the house or lot they prefer, so they can envision themselves living there.

To offset any lingering doubts, you could show them alternatives which are less desirable. Find ways to remove any features of their preferred selection which they do not like. Solve any problems which arise in completing the transaction.

When everything has been discussed and you feel the right time has arrived, ask them for their approval to close the sale.

Signing the contract is not the end of the sales person's job. There may be other problems to solve, setbacks to overcome and details to handle before the transaction is completely finished. Customers do not like to be abandoned by sales people. They expect continuing interest in them, and help if needed. By providing this on-going support and making sure customers are satisfied, the salesman develops a good professional reputation and lays the foundation for future sales.

CHAPTER 16

"MOTIVATING PEOPLE"

One View of Motivation

In a sense, management and motivation come to the same thing. Managers must get employees to perform tasks that they are not spontaneously inclined to do.

In another sense, no one can ever "motivate" anyone to do anything. If a person does not want what you have to offer, then there is little you can do to *make* him or her want to act.

Motives are those desires and wants which cause action. Hence, "motivating people" means causing them to want to do something or intensifying a want sufficiently to cause action in the appropriate direction.

Some of the most powerful motives are inborn. These include hunger, thirst, fatigue, fear, sex and other purely biological drives. Other motives are learned, such as the desire for a particular kind of food, a particular marital partner, a beer on a hot day, and so on. Most motives are combinations of inborn needs and learned desires.

Some objects of desire are wanted because of what they are; others are wanted because they lead to something else. As a matter of practical fact, intrinsic properties of the methods used must be evaluated along with the attractions of the goal. Ends do not justify the means if the negative characteristics of the means offset the advantages of the objectives.

Motivational Theories

Many, many, many theories of motivation have been formulated. The early Greek and Roman philosophers had fairly sophisticated ideas about what causes people to act. Since then, every school of psychology has contributed its particular motivational concepts. Contemporary theories come from many academic disciplines, both theoretical and applied.

One way to put the multiplicity of theoretical entities into perspective is to imagine the task of organizing a collection of miscellaneous objects. There would be an almost limitless number of ways to group the objects. You could put together all that were the same color, or the same weight, or were near each other, or were made of similar material, and so on.

Now imagine that these objects represent different human motives (wants). The many theories of motivation can be seen as simply different ways of grouping these motives. For example, one theory may put desire for a new car in the same group as desire for an education; another may not.

This suggests that we would be wise not to take any one theory of motivation too seriously. Rather, let us learn from each and use each where it proves most helpful.

Some of the better-known motivational theories are listed below.

1. *Religious views* from ancient times to the present have emphasized the motives of good and evil. "Good" is usually equated with actions devoted to worship of the deity, helping other people of the same faith, and resistance to desires of physical gratification.

A problem always encountered by this type of view is that the different religions have differing ideas on what is good and what people should be allowed or required to do. A person regarded as "good" by some religions may be judged as "evil" by others. A person may consider himself to be good simply because he stands by his religious convictions. Because other religions are different, such behavior is automatically evil to them.

Hence, the suspicion arises that motivational views of religious origin may be primarily attempts by "true believers" to impose their beliefs on others.

2. *Sigmund Freud* and his followers believed that people are motivated by their animal appetites, modified by socially-learned restraints. For example, the sexual drive is controlled by social customs and rules. This situation leads to internal conflicts, as each person tries to satisfy both the drive and the restraining rules.

Many subsequent psychological formulations have followed the general framework of Freud's theory, which itself resembled the psychological philosophies of Plato and Aristotle. Most contemporary theorists regard Freud as correct in many of his insights, but as mistaken in overemphasizing the role of repressed sexual appetite and the power of self-awareness to cure psychological disorders.

3. *Behavioristic psychologists* argued for two levels of motivation: the Primary Drives, which are unlearned and largely innate (hunger, sex, etc.), and Secondary Drives, which are learned motives derived from their association with the satisfaction of primary drives. Thus, desire for food (hunger) would be a primary drive, but desire for a hamburger with catsup, relish and onion is a secondary drive, learned when the sandwich in question was associated in the past with satisfaction of the primary hunger drive.

Doubt has been thrown on the Behaviorists' theories because they have been unable to prove that all secondary drives are learned in the way described, and because some non-primary drives exist for which there has been no opportunity for learning.

4. *David McClelland* contributed the concept of "Achievement Motivation," which is the need to accomplish recognizable goals. His studies contrasted this need with a desire to be liked and accepted, the "Affiliation Need," and found that highly achievement-motivated persons were often low in need for affiliation, and vice versa. He found that business and government leaders generally score high on tests for achievement motivation.

5. *"Cognitive Dissonance"* as a motive was first described by Festinger and Eckerman. This motive makes people try to resolve conflicts between their beliefs. For example, a desire or expectation of significant achievement could come into conflict with recognition of non-achievement. According to the cognitive dissonance theory, the person will then act or think in a way that would reduce this conflict. He might stop what he was doing and pursue another goal, deny that there was any conflict, delude

himself into believing that he would be promoted soon, or otherwise remove the problem from his mind.

6. *Expectancy Theory* is similar. It says that a person's attitudes and actions are a function of their utility in bringing about desired outcomes and in the evaluation of those outcomes. A person must believe that his efforts will be sufficient to qualify as a good performance and that this performance will lead to something valued.

7. *Abraham Maslow's* theory placed motives into a hierarchy:

On the first (lowest level) are Physiological Needs;

On the second level are Security Needs;

On the third level are Social Needs;

On the fourth level are Ego Needs;

On the top level are Self-actualization Needs.

He says that people will be motivated by the lower needs until these are sufficiently satisfied. Then, they will seek to satisfy the higher-level needs.

Managers have generally found Maslow's theory to be very useful. It keeps them from assuming that all employees or customers are motivated by only one or two things. However, there are still questions for the theory, such as, "Why do people sometimes violate the order of the hierarchy?" "Why does a soldier sacrifice physiological and security needs to go into battle, even to the extent of losing his life?" "Where do adventure, pleasure and knowledge fit into the hierarchy?" "How do we categorize complex motives, such as desire for a big, luxurious house in the country?"

8. *Douglas McGregor's* research and consulting experience led him to make a now-famous distinction between managers who believed in "Theory X" and "Theory Y." Theory X managers think that workers are

lazy, do not like work, will not work unless forced to do so by overpowering needs, must be given frequent and specific instructions, and must be closely supervised. Theory Y managers believe that people are not like that: they will perform willingly if given the right incentives, they want to do useful work, they often want more responsibility, and they can direct themselves.

McGregor's distinction between Theory X and Theory Y can be correlated with Maslow's motivational system. A Theory X manager would be one who believed that workers are motivated only by the lower-level motives; a Theory Y manager, one who believed that workers are moved by the higher-level motives as well. A Theory X manager is more autocratic; a Theory Y manager, more democratic.

Research has shown that application of Theory Y does work better in many organizations. A Theory X management style works better in other organizations. These findings have led various authors to formulate "Theory Z" and other alternative theories.

Perhaps "Contingency Theory" says it best: use the motivational theory and management style that yields the best results in your situation. There is no one style which is always best in all circumstances.

9. *Frederick Herzberg* studied what makes people happy or unhappy with their jobs. He found that "satisfiers" and "dissatisfaction removers" are not the same. Employees' dissatisfaction with low wages, for instance, can be removed by a raise in pay, but a feeling of real job satisfaction comes only if something is accomplished by the employees or they enjoy their work or both. Management will never make workers happy by just removing dissatisfactions. It must also provide opportunities for

workers to gain satisfactions actively: from the work itself, by doing jobs they enjoy and can do well, by personal achievement and by pride in performance.

10.*Other theories* of motivation have been derived from the study of psychiatry, interpersonal relationships, social and group dynamics, and industrial and consumer psychology.

You should use whichever of these theories have the most utility for you. Remember that no theory is the *only* correct one.

In fact, any attempt to establish one theory of motivation as superior to all others should be viewed with suspicion. This is because motivational hierarchies are also value hierarchies. If someone says one motive is "higher," "better," or otherwise superior to another, this suggests that the motive is also morally better. Implications of moral superiority are beyond the reach of factual and scientific inquiry. Theories embodying such hierarchies may be thinly-disguised attempts to promote the speaker's value system.

Major Obstacles to "Motivating"

One obstacle to motivating others is that you may be unable to create the conditions which would be necessary. If people have no wants which you can help them satisfy, or if the rewards you can provide are "not worth it" for the time and effort they would have to provide, then you *cannot* motivate them, no matter how much upper management insists that you must. To motivate others over the long term, you need the ability to deliver consistent rewards of sufficient quality and quantity.

Another obstacle is determining what particular people want. Motives are not the same for all. Many times, when you have no success with someone, it is because you are offering a benefit he does not really want or are failing to help him toward his real goals.

How to "Motivate" People

1. First, Find Out What People Want.
   - Ask them. This is the easiest way, when done properly.
   - Guess what people want on the basis of their age, sex, background, etc. For example, younger people frequently want new experiences; older people often desire security or stability.
   - Judge by their behavior. Suppose an employee declares her strong desire to get ahead in her career, but spends all her freetime in social activities, misses work frequently, and never volunteers for extra assignments. Her behavior is probably a better indicator of her real motivation (to have fun).
   - Assume that everyone has some of the most widespread wants. Almost everybody wants to be liked by others, to do interesting and significant work, to be well rewarded, and so forth.
   - Check your assumptions and conclusions. Because motives are hard to judge and may change, you should seek frequent "feedback" (confirmation) of your estimates. See if the person's behavior verifies your predictions. You can calculate the strength of a motive by observing how much trouble or pain he will endure in order to satisfy it.

2. Then, Apply Your Knowledge of Their Wants.

Motivate people by giving them opportunities to satisfy those wants.

3. Create New Motives In People By Providing New Experiences.

Some motives are created by inborn mechanisms; others, by experience; most, by combinations of the two.

We can do little about inborn mechanisms, but we can provide new experiences. The Law of Effect tells us that any behavior which is perceived as leading to a pleasurable outcome will be repeated, and that the opposite applies to a behavior leading to an unpleasant result. Therefore, to get a person to want to do something, have him try it and make sure his effort leads to a positive outcome. Or, have him try the opposite of this behavior (usually, omitting the behavior) and allow an unpleasant outcome to follow. The effect will be a growth of motivation toward the desired behavior.

Applications of this strategy would include

- *showing* him the item, product or action in a realistic situation (this is common in television commercials);
- having him *try* the item, product or action;
- having the benefits *described* as vividly as possible by those who have experienced them;
- getting him to *imagine* himself trying the item and enjoying it, or lacking the item and not enjoying it.

Reward those actions, attitudes and motives which you want; punish or fail to reward those you do not want. For example, you could smile and be friendly toward those who are doing a good job, but frown or be "cool" toward those that fail to do their best. Let those who do not perform well experience the full negative consequences of their poor performance, including a lack of praise and less reward than that received by other employees. Do the opposite for good performers.

Introduce extra rewards for new or harder tasks. People do not welcome changes in routines because they must alter their habitual behaviors. Once initial resistance has been overcome, however, they will accept methods which are better, easier or lead to greater reward.

As the Law of Effect points out, people will become positively motivated toward anything which leads to pleasant, rewarding results. To build motive strength, provide repeated experiences of such rewards.

Achievement Motivation can be strengthened through the Law of Effect. Although everyone has some achievement motivation, those strongest in this motive often accomplish more in their careers. They get ahead because they have the need to get ahead. (Success requires more than motivation, of course. It calls for knowledge, skill, talent, persistence and even some luck.)

There are obvious advantages to being highly achievement motivated. The motive provides a constant urge toward useful action. It strengthens other constructive motives. It has some disadvantages, as well. Too much achievement need can cause stress (from an unrelenting drive to excel), difficulty in enjoying other facets of life, impatience, and inability to appreciate differing points of view. On balance, however, the advantages outweigh the disadvantages for most people and most management situations.

You can increase achievement motivation in your employees, your children or yourself. McClelland himself developed effective training programs. The key is to always reward successful achievement efforts and fail to reward failures or lack of trying.

Begin by arranging a succession of tasks for your employees or others under your direction. Each task should be challenging, but not too difficult. All or most should result in success. When this happens, immediately recognize and reward it. If a failure occurs, do not provide the reward but be sure that the person succeeds at the next several tasks. This teaches her not to give up in the face of failure and that success will come if she keeps trying.

As time goes by, difficulty of assigned tasks should be increased. This maintains a sense of challenge and a pride in accomplishment. Intensify the satisfaction realized from success by providing praise, recognition and reward.

4. Create New Wants By Building On Existing Wants.

Arousing interest, covered in an earlier chapter, is one method of motivating. We create the feeling of interest by showing how an action can lead to a desired outcome. Gaining Cooperation and Persuading also use existing wants to trigger constructive action.

Another way to build on existing wants is to use them in arousing strong emotions. These emotions are powerful stimulants to action. For example, a sales representative may know that you want a new car, but she will be unable to sell you one until she can strengthen your immediate "feeling-like-buying-it" enough to trigger your action. Sales people themselves are motivated by increasing their "feeling-like-selling" — through sales meetings, motivational talks, incentives and other forms of encouragement.

Because feelings are not stable, they must be re-kindled frequently. This type of motivation is best used where temporary level of feeling is critical. It is generally ineffective where sustained, long-term effort is required.

Other emotions which motivate on a short-term basis are excitement, enthusiasm, joy, ambition, desire, passion, anger, jealousy, pride, acceptance, belonging, affection, appreciation, fear, admiration, comfort, boredom, restlessness, impatience, obligation and gratitude. Social pressure can create strong emotions, through the approval or disapproval of the group. It is commonly used to motivate individuals toward group goals and standards.

SUMMARY

There have been many theories of motivation. You can motivate people by (1) Creating New Wants Through New Experiences, following the Law of Effect, or (2) Arousing Emotions Based on Existing Wants. Design reward and punishment systems carefully, to encourage desired behavior and discourage unwanted behavior. Use the Law of Effect to develop Achievement Motivation. To trigger actions, arouse initiating emotions such as interest, desire, social acceptance and enthusiasm.

APPLICATIONS

These questions will test your ability to apply material in this chapter. See if you can answer them.

1. "Could you use methods of 'Motivating People' to motivate yourself?"

Yes! Begin by analyzing your motives as revealed in your behavior. Also consider motives you may possess because of your age, sex, background, etc. Assume that you have the motives typical of most human beings in similar circumstances, unless you have strong reasons to believe you do not.

Motivate yourself by seeking out new experiences. Enroll in courses, meet new people, read books, travel, try different projects in your business. Set goals for yourself and reward yourself when you meet them. Keep up your enthusiasm by talking to other people about your hopes and plans. Work with others. Put yourself in positions where you must succeed or suffer the consequences.

2. "How can you get people motivated toward teamwork instead of wanting to work alone or competing with each other destructively? How can you get employees to accept direction?"

The former question is the easier. People pursue objectives which are rewarded. Therefore, when individual effort is rewarded over cooperation, individual effort will predominate. If you want more teamwork, then team results must be the basis for reward. Do not compensate employees on their individual performance alone; reward them for their teams' performance. Many incentive systems, from profit sharing to profit centers, are designed with this result in mind.

Acceptance of authority is difficult for many. Taking directions from another is inherently unattractive. People who do this willingly do so because they believe they are better off than if they resist. People will also accept authority if they agreed to that when they accepted their jobs, if they trust and respect those in charge, and if they understand the reasons for orders. It helps greatly if the product or service provided by the organization is recognized as important and worthwhile.

3. "What new experiences could you provide people in your department that might motivate them toward better performance? What emotions would be most useful in motivating your employees?"

Here are some possibilities:

Job rotation, job enrichment, incentives, production teams, quality circles, management attention, educational incentives, seminars, democratic management, competition for positions, work standards, top management visits, delegation of authority, centralization of authority, an employee stock ownership plan, social activities, company sports teams, lay-offs, corporate growth and subsequent advancement opportunity, reductions in the work-force and/or amount of compensation as required by economic conditions or the company's competitive position, "pep talks," motivational speakers, employee performance reviews, etc.

EXAMPLES

1. "How can we motivate people in our organization to do excellent instead of just passable work?"
What is your answer?

Discussion: What is considered passable and what excellent will depend upon the standards used. Standards can be raised, of course, but workers may resist. One solution is to convince employees that the present production rates are too low. Information from comparable companies could be used. Another approach is to provide additional benefits in return for meeting the new, higher standards. An inexpensive reward you can always give is recognition. Pride in work is a powerful incentive. Encourage it through the public acknowledgement of excellent performance. Some people will perform better in hopes of advancement. This cannot be offered to everyone, however. In general, financial reward is still the most potent of all incentives to work.

It is unrealistic to think that top performance will be achieved at all times. People can do wonders over a short period, but that is not to say they can maintain this level day after day or week after week. Permanent improvement in performance levels almost always requires more than a motivational increase; it requires new methods, better equipment or job reorganization.

2. "We want to implement a company-wide motivation plan. It should work for all departments and all levels, from lowest-level clerks to the chief executive. What kind of plan will provide what we need?"
What is your answer?

Discussion: The plan can certainly be company-wide, but no one set of incentives can be applied equally across the board. People at the various levels and in different departments will have differing needs, wants and expectations.

For example, those in entry-level and unskilled jobs may be most interested in just having a decent job. They need to earn a reasonable living; they want pleasant work

and good working conditions. Motivate their performance and loyalty by paying them more than they can
obtain elsewhere for similar work, treat them better than
they would be treated elsewhere, and provide whatever
other rewards you can.

Some people in lower or entry-level positions will
want to move up into better jobs. Many in middle
management or skilled positions will want to advance.
Motivate each by providing them opportunities for
promotion, greater responsibility, more flexibility, and
better compensation. Allow employees to compete with
each other for advancements. Provide opportunities for
personal and professional development.

Top executives will not be motivated by incentives
appropriate for other people in the organization, for the
simple reason that they already have these things. They
have sufficient income, responsibility, flexibility, influence and position. The chief executive cannot even
advance.

Motivation of top management is done by the "stick
and carrot" technique. The "stick" is lack of job security
if performance is not satisfactory. Most chief executives
can be dismissed by the board of directors, at any time.
The "carrot" is substantial financial reward, usually
through performance-based bonuses or stock options,
and an increase of power and influence which a successful organization brings to its upper managers. When
management also owns the corporation, there is an automatic reward whenever the company prospers.

If your organization employs academic or medical
professionals, scientists, architects, engineers, or other
highly-trained employees, you will need a basic understanding of the professional values and standards of

these specialists. They usually want independence to direct their own work, colleagues with whom to discuss ideas, adequate equipment and assistance for their projects, respect and recognition. A successful manager will find ways to satisfy these needs.

Two perennial problems for all motivational systems are (1) the difficulty of measuring performance and correlating it with reward, and (2) the tendency for any incentive to "get old," that is, less motivating to people who become used to receiving the benefits or no longer want them at all.

Measuring individual performance is difficult for jobs which are obviously important to the whole organization but which have little measurable effect on the product. For example, how do you measure the effect of a personnel director on a finished automobile or appliance? How does a good corporate secretary help sell the hamburgers of a restaurant chain? It is possible to make up ways to judge performance for these positions, but their direct relevance to the "bottom line" may be hard to prove.

For some occupations, performance can be measured, but there are multiple objectives. These may be in conflict. Is a successful teacher one whose students achieve the highest test scores, is best educated in her teaching field, has the fewest discipline problems, is most popular with pupils, or is best liked by co-workers and the administration?

Even when job performance can be easily evaluated, reward cannot always be correlated with it. For example, computer systems analysts have recently been in great demand. To keep one, you may have to pay more than for other managers, even if performance is poor. Or, if your company is in economic difficulty, you may have to reduce pay for everyone. This will result in inadequate compensation for those who have performed well and obviously deserve much more.

Any incentive can become "old." Counter this by reminding employees of what they are receiving. Temporary loss of a benefit can dramatize its value. Adjust rewards as people advance, as they age, and as new wants take priority over old ones.

Some motivators can be company-wide. Pride in the organization is one. This should be encouraged by consistent and sustained campaigns to support the corporate image. A good organizational image can have a positive effect on potential customers, community members, government regulators, and investors, as well as employees.

Other possible company-wide motivators include universally-accepted values and objectives, fair rewards in return for contributions (Some companies have been criticized for over-compensating top executives compared with other employees.), feelings of teamwork and respect for individuals throughout the organization.

Some references for theories mentioned in this chapter:

Festinger, Leon. A Theory of Cognitive Dissonance. Row, Peterson, Evanston, IL, 1957.

Freud, Sigmund. An Outline of Psychoanalysis. Norton, New York, 1940.

Herzberg, Frederick. Work and the Nature of Man. World, Cleveland, 1966.

Maslow, Abraham. "A Theory of Human Motivation."

Psychological Review, 50, 1943.

McClelland, David C., et al. The Achievement Motive. Appleton-Century-Crofts, New York, 1960.

McGregor, Douglas. The Human Side of Management. McGraw-Hill, New York, 1960.

Vroom, Victor. Work and Motivation. John Wiley & Sons, New York, 1964.

Watson, John. Behaviorism. Norton, New York, 1925.

CHAPTER 17

CORRECTING FAULTS IN YOURSELF AND OTHERS

Problems Caused by Faults and Bad Habits

Bad habits and other personal faults can offset all of a person's good characteristics. Sometimes, just one defect of character or behavior will cause us to fail completely. Other people may regard our flaws as so offensive that they judge us on these alone.

We may be completely unaware of our own faults. Because we hold generally favorable opinions of ourselves, we tend to discount the importance of any "minor" weaknesses. Other people do not have this reason for overlooking our failings, especially if these interfere with their interests.

Even when we are conscious of our defects, we may be unable to correct them. Some inborn characteristics are impossible to change. Bad habits can be painful to over-come, especially if we have practiced them for a long time and gain great satisfaction from them. Habitual actions can become so automatic that we have done them before we have a chance to resist.

Causes

A habit is any behavior pattern acquired by repetition in the presence of reward or punishment. It is charac-terized by regularity, predictability, ease of performance, decreased power of resistance, and by becoming auto-matic or involuntary.

Generally, the longer a habit has persisted and the greater the satisfaction received, the stronger it is. You can safely assume that anyone with a habit is receiving some reward from that behavior. If you want to change the behavior, you must remove or counteract the reward.

Whether or not a behavior is a fault or a virtue may be in dispute. Each of us has characteristics with which we are satisfied but which annoy other people. To us, these are not faults; to them, they are.

Should you pay attention to the opinions of others regarding your behavior? The best answer seems to be, "Yes and No." "Yes," you should pay attention if they will act on their opinions in a way that could harm you. "No," if the behavior is so important to you that you are willing to put up with their negative reactions.

Some faults are unavoidable or not worth the effort to change. The answer then is to learn to live with them.

How To Correct Faults In Others

The title of this section should be "How to *Attempt* to Correct Faults in Others," to emphasize that it is often very hard to do. Consider your own bad habits. You recognize them to be unproductive, but you still have not dropped them. Maybe you have tried to quit and failed, or maybe you do not really want to change. Perhaps you know of no effective way to change. Now imagine how hard it would be for someone else to get you to alter your behavior, when you yourself have been unable to do so. The same thing applies when you contemplate changing a behavior problem in another person. If it were easy to do, the person would have done it himself. If he does not want to change, then he will resist.

This is not to say that it is impossible, just that you should be prepared for difficulties and less-than-perfect results.

Here are three methods which will give you a good chance for success.

Method #1: Correcting Faults Through Persuasion
Follow these five steps:
- Gain the person's favorable attention to you and to the problem.
- Gain his confidence, if necessary.
- Cause the person to become dissatisfied with his behavior and determined to change it; show him what the cost will be to him if he continues; make him unhappy with his present behavior.
- Working with him, seek an effective method for changing; formulate a practical plan for doing so; get him to decide that this is the best thing for him to do.

- Intensify his feeling-like-changing by pointing out the rewards for acting and the dangers of inaction; provide support for his efforts; offset any of his excuses for not performing as he has decided; keep encouraging his efforts and discouraging any attempts to give up.

As an example, consider how you would persuade someone to quit smoking. You could get his attention by dramatizing the effects of tobacco smoke. You could gain his confidence by showing your concern for him and your ability to help. You could make him unhappy with the health problems he is going to experience if he does not quit. You could try to scare him. You could say that other people will not tolerate it any longer.

You would then help him find a method for quitting, one which will work for him. You would continue to encourage him and watch for any tendency toward reversion.

Help him combat these two temptations: Saying, "I cannot do it"; and Being unwilling to make the necessary changes. The former is just an attempt to back out of the decision when the going gets tough. The latter expresses the understandable desire to realize the benefits without taking the difficult steps to reach them. Defeating a well-entrenched habit may require changing many other behaviors that support that habit.

An addictive behavior, such as smoking, is especially difficult to alter. One proven rule is *not* to decide to stop forever; instead, decide not to do it "this time." Decide that every time and the problem is solved. This procedure counteracts the tendency to excuse exceptions. It emphasizes that an undesirable habit must be overcome instance by instance.

A warning: when attempting to correct faults in other people, do not expect it to be an enjoyable experience for either you or them. You must prepare yourself for unpleasantness as they react negatively to your efforts. Be ready to be direct (blunt) with them, if it becomes necessary. Tell the person what his undesirable behavior is doing to hurt *you*, and what it is going to cost *him* if he does not stop. He may not have realized, until now, how seriously his behavior is regarded by others. He will realize it when he sees that it could cause him to be demoted, transferred, docked in pay or dismissed. Tell him. He needs to know.

When conducting a correctional interview, do not criticize the person. Criticize the behavior only. Make clear at all times that you value him as a person and have every confidence in his ability to improve.

Method #2: Correcting Faults Through Application of Differential Rewards and Punishments.

Use the Law of Effect. Arrange working conditions so that people are consistently rewarded for desired behavior; eliminate any rewards being received for undesired habits.

Check the working conditions in your department. Are people always rewarded for doing good work, or are they sometimes punished? They may be punished deliberately by other workers, who put on pressure for exceeding the usual performance norms. They can also be punished by the structure of the situation. For example, a secretary is supposed to "look busy," even if she does not have enough to do. With little to do, there is no reason for her to work efficiently. Naturally, she will work slower. This allows her to look busy with the work she has. She may even make mistakes so she can use up some of her idle time in correcting them. To correct this "fault" of inefficient work, just provide her with more to do.

The following are methods psychologists use to help people overcome undesirable habits. You can apply the same techniques in helping your employees overcome their bad habits. These methods work by (1) removing whatever rewards are being received for the undesirable behavior, (2) providing a new behavior to take its place, and (3) differentially reinforcing each over a period of time.

The Incompatible Response Method introduces a response which is impossible to perform at the same time as the undesired behavior. For example, suppose someone likes to be in charge of projects, but does not like to do the necessary careful supervision or paying attention to details. You can make the one dependent on the other. Put the individual in charge of the daily supervision, including attention to details. Her desire to be in charge should overcome her dislike for close attention. She will learn to do it, because she cannot otherwise be in control. (A possible danger is that her dislike of details could overcome her desire for control. To offset this, gradually increase the amount of careful supervision she would have to do.)

The Exhaustive Method first exercises the undesirable habit until it is overdone and therefore no longer pleasurable. Then, a new behavior is elicited and rewarded. For instance, desire to smoke cigarettes may be lowest and most easily broken after smoking too many. To cure a manager of trying to do everything himself, you might wait until he has exhausted himself getting out all the yearly reports alone. Then he may welcome your suggestion that he delegate some of his work.

The Toleration Method takes stimuli which normally trigger the undesired response and matches them to a new, desired reaction. Thus, a person who smokes when nervous could be made just a little nervous and given gum to chew. Smoking is not compatible with the new response of chewing gum. Over time, the impulse to smoke when nervous would be replaced by the new, better response.

Aversion Therapy is another name for punishment. It works best when an alternative behavior is rewarded at the same time. It does little good to punish a behavior if that is the only response available to a person. Provide and reward a new desirable response at the same time the old response is punished. This allows an outlet for the motivation underlying the action. The original Boys' Clubs are an example. Located in the poorer neighborhoods of large cities, these athletic associations gave boys an alternative to the pursuit of crime and life on the streets.

Punishment always causes problems, because of the resentment it creates. The *only* time it should be used is when another possibility for behavior is provided and rewarded, and when other methods have proven ineffective.

A practice which is usually ineffective is a mere change of scene. It does not "cure" a person to be sent away for a day, a week or a month. Even if the problem behavior disappears in the different setting, it is likely to reappear once he or she returns to the set of circumstances which triggered and rewarded it before.

Method #3: Accepting and Adjusting

This method is really a non-method. It says, "Do not worry too much about what a person cannot do. Concentrate on what he can do. Find ways to help him use the abilities he has to benefit himself and others."

Imagine a great opera singer whose family criticized her because she was not good at bookkeeping, sales, management, or painting? This would be absurd, would it not? A great singer does not need to be good at these other things. Yet, you may be doing the same type of thinking about your employees. You may be so focused on some of their inabilities that you fail to recognize their unique abilities. Find out what each can do best. Put their talents to constructive use. This is the wise use of human potential, an important part of every manager's job.

By the way, the same applies to you. You earn your living because of what you do well. Try to improve in areas of weakness, of course. Mostly, however, concentrate on your strengths. Develop those talents and abilities that will allow you to accomplish the most.

How To Correct Faults In Yourself

To make the most of your capabilities, decide first on your long-term goals. Then adopt a program of self-improvement.

Benjamin Franklin kept a list of qualities he wanted to have. Periodically, he would rate himself on these qualities and work on those most in need of improvement.

William James suggested that we should act as if we already had the attributes we wished to have. If you want to be at ease with people instead of shy, he would advise you to act as if you were at ease, even when you do not feel that way. The appropriate feelings will follow when you see that you can be successful.

If you are evaluated on your performance at work (and aren't we all?), then grade yourself in advance using the same methods. Select areas for improvement and work on them. Chart your progress.

Warning! It is easy to delude yourself when your self-esteem is at stake. If you have a fault and recognize it, you have only one fault, but if you fail to acknowledge it, you have two faults.

To achieve greater peace of mind, apply the following categorization technique. For every bad habit or behavior you wish you did not have, decide whether you are going to eliminate it or not. If so, select an effective method and get rid of it. If not, decide to accept it and live with it. Why torture yourself with guilt feelings over things you are not going to do anything to correct?

Develop good habits. Use them to replace undesirable ones. For example, by developing a habit of hard work, you will not only achieve more, but you will find difficult tasks easier because you will be used to them. Other good habits to develop are eating sensibly, getting enough exercise and rest, and avoiding addictive substances.

As you repeat these useful behaviors, they will become much easier. As you avoid the destructive ones, those habits will weaken. The key to success is consistency.

SUMMARY

Personal faults and bad habits are not easy to change, whether in another person or in yourself. Two methods to use are Persuasion and Applications of the Law of Effect. The former involves a face-to-face conversation in which you persuade the person to change. This may not be pleasant at all times. The latter requires restructuring of the situation so that desirable behavior is rewarded and undesirable behavior is not. Learn to recognize and utilize people's strengths, even if you cannot correct all their faults.

APPLICATIONS

List your most serious faults and bad habits. Identify the causes of each and the rewards you are receiving from them. For each of these, decide if you really want to change. If you do not, quit worrying about it and accept the behavior. If you do want to change, formulate an effective plan and carry it out.

Consider faults in someone with whom you work. Is this person's performance your responsibility? Can you change his behavior? Would it be worth the effort? If the answers are "Yes," use the methods described above to correct it. If the answers are "No," decide how you will change *your* reactions to this person. What will you do to keep the behavior from bothering you and from interfering with your own and other employee's performance?

As a practice exercise, make a detailed plan of how you would persuade someone you know to change a behavior. Also, plan how you would change working conditions to eliminate an undesirable habit in one of your employees.

EXAMPLES

1. "Gerald is an engineer in my company. He is habitually late with everything he does. He comes to work late. He returns late from vacation. He falls behind other

engineers on joint projects. Worst of all, he turns in assignments and reports way beyond the deadlines.

This is not a minor problem. It is costing us money and causes unending difficulties. It is creating a morale problem with the other engineers who are on time with their work. If I cannot get Gerald to change, I am going to have to let him go. What can I do to correct his perpetual lateness?"

What is your answer?

Discussion: There are people like this. In some cases, they lose job after job and still do not improve.

Assuming that the present problem is not insolvable, the better approach would be to use persuasion. Call the engineer into your office. Explain the problem to him, emphasizing the serious consequences to you and the company which justify your concern. Then, tell him that he must change or you will have to let him go.

If he wants to keep his job, you have now both gained his attention and aroused his interest. The next step is to work with him to find a solution. One method to get him to work on time would be to devise a better early-morning schedule and have him stick to it. You might put him in a car pool, have an answering service call him at a sufficiently early hour, or even get his wife to help, if she will. (A similar method was used by a Detroit company which was trying to give disadvantaged youths a chance for steady employment. They found that the reason many were not reporting to work on time was that they did not own alarm clocks. The company bought them some.)

You also need a method which will ensure that his reports are in by the deadlines. You might require regular progress reports. If he fell behind on any of these, there would still be time to catch up. These progress reports would also make him aware of where he was at frequent intervals. (Use a similar device to keep yourself moving on work where you tend to become "bogged down." Set a timer for regular intervals, such as a half hour. The alarm will make you conscious of the passage of time.)

Another method would be to team him with an efficient engineer. Of course, you will run some risk of ruining the good engineer, instead of having the good one cure the bad one!

It is possible that you will not want to spend this much time working with him on these methods. You or he or both of you may feel that it is up to him alone to find a way to change his behavior. If you decide to take this approach, make the situation clear to him and set a deadline for his correction of the problem. Then, if he is unable to do it, you will have no choice but to terminate him.

2. "A woman in our office is a problem because of her negative attitude. She complains about everything and everyone. She never takes any initiative or accepts any responsibility herself. She always 'puts down' the efforts of others, so everybody hates her.

How can we get her to be more positive?"
What is your answer?

Discussion: Believe it or not, studies of group effectiveness show that it is *good* to have a critic in the organization. The critic keeps people from being carried away by ideas which are not really very good but which enjoy the support of a popular majority. You should not eliminate all negative thinkers. They may save your business!

Even so, if you have decided that the person's utility is not worth the aggravations, there are two approaches you could try.

First, you could put the person in charge of a project or job. It is impossible to be totally negative about everything and still get things done. (Note that professional critics do not produce the kind of works they critique.)

Second, you could tell the person that she has a right to her opinions but that she is not allowed to *express* negative thoughts on the job because of the detrimental effect they have on morale and, therefore, on company results. This is your legitimate concern as the manager. You have a right to demand behavior which promotes the group's goals. (The courts have upheld the rights of management in similar cases. An airline flight attendant was dismissed when he refused to ever smile. He sued for improper dismissal, but he lost. The court found that this was a legitimate requirement of the job because it had a significant effect upon the satisfaction of passengers and the success of the airline.)

Third, you could find ways to use this person's characteristics and abilities for mutual advantage. She might like working alone and perform an independent job very well in order to keep it. She might make an excellent auditor, quality-control inspector or internal investigator.

3. "The boss says I drink too much. He says if I don't quit, he will either fire me or send me to one of those 'rehabilitation' programs. What can I do?"
What is your answer?

Discussion: This could be a trick question. What does the employee mean when he asks, "What can I do?" Does he mean, "What can I do to quit drinking?" or does he mean, "What can I do to keep my job and stay out of the rehabilitation program while continuing to drink as before?"

Addicted drinkers usually mean the latter. That is why they do not respond well to suggestions about how to quit the habit. From their point of view, you would have missed the point if you gave such advice.

Some alcoholics can overcome the habit themselves, by an act of will power; some can be scared into quitting; but, most will require professional help.

CHAPTER 18

AVOIDING FRUSTRATION, IRRITATION AND ANGER

The Problem

Frustration, irritation and anger are unpleasant emotions. They can rob life of its reasonable enjoyment. They can turn people bitter. They can distort thinking, disrupt friendships and destroy good will.

In addition, they are often useless, leading to no beneficial action at all but only destructive impulses and rash behavior.

Even though these emotions are widely recognized as generally useless and sometimes dangerous, many people cannot keep from experiencing them. They do not know how to avoid irritation and anger. Once angry, they do not know how to control it.

Individuals with high frustration levels and quick tempers tend to blame circumstances and other people for anything that goes wrong. They develop habits of being irritated, of blaming others, of "blowing off steam" whenever they feel like it, and of oversimplifying complex problems into "me against them" thinking.

For those who want to do so, there are plenty of excuses for losing control. Anger is a natural reaction to threatening or frustrating occurrences, and there are always people and situations which we do not like. Even if everything is going well, we can become impatient over the rate of progress.

People with anger and irritation problems may still blame external factors, even when they themselves are obviously the cause of the problem. Rather than say, "I dropped and broke it," they would say, "It got dropped and broken" or "You (or something) made me drop it."

Frustration, irritation and anger are not always bad. They are beneficial when they motivate us to take needed action. We should learn to recognize when strong emotions may lead to destructive actions or excess stress, and when they are beneficial goads to action.

Causes

The feelings of frustration, irritation and anger are caused by beliefs. Frustration is caused by the belief, "I am not getting what I want," or "I am not getting what I want fast enough or easy enough." Irritation is caused by the belief, "I do not like this; I wish it were gone." Anger is caused by the belief, "I hate this and he (she, it) has no right to do this to me."

Frustration, irritation or anger may result from (1) situations which make our desires impossible to satisfy,

(2) active interference by other people, or (3) conflicts of motives within ourselves. The first of these is generally easiest to accept. The second is the cause of much inter-personal trouble and ill-feeling. The third can be the most serious: it makes a person unhappy and unsure of himself; unresolved, it can lead to serious emotional problems.

The basic causes of frustration, irritation and anger are
- failure to expect undesired situations, and
- inability to solve the problems.

We become frustrated when we see that our desires are not being satisfied, despite our best efforts. We become irritated whenever something happens which we did not expect and which we have no plans to handle. Likewise, we become angry when we are "too stupid to think of anything useful to do."

Consider: You would not become frustrated or angry if you could immediately solve your problems. Also, you would not become angry if you knew in advance that a problem was going to arise.

Lack of realistic expectations and inability to cope are the root causes of frustration, irritation and anger.

In this light, it is hard to understand how anyone could be proud of a hot temper. Since such people do exist, we know that they must be receiving some kind of reward from their habitual frustration and anger. Perhaps they feel proud of themselves because they are "tough" and "can take it." Perhaps they like the image they project. Maybe they are using anger to frighten or control others. Some may be exhibiting anger to dramatize their problems and gain sympathy.

When individuals become frustrated, they often resort to "Displaced Aggression" to relieve some of the stress. This occurs when they cannot act against whatever is causing the frustration, such as a boss. Instead, they take aggressive action against those who are totally blameless but who cannot defend themselves, such as a spouse or children. (Some people even kick their dogs!)

Possible Solutions

1. Changing Your Attitude Toward Irritation and Anger

You will never conquer anger if you believe it is natural, acceptable, or something of which to be proud. To counter this tendency, try this: The next time you feel yourself becoming angry, imagine yourself as a big baby, lying in a crib, screaming for your mother to come and make you happy. This image will remind you that temper is an infantile mechanism for solving problems which the child cannot solve for himself. As an adult, you are expected to do better than this.

2. Eliminating False and Useless Beliefs

Frustration, irritation and anger are usually caused by unreasonable beliefs about the world and the people in it. These beliefs lead to false expectations, which are bound to be contradicted by reality.

Following are some false beliefs which commonly trigger angry reactions.

*   "Having a hot temper is something of which to be proud."

Actually, it is childish and stupid.

*   "Frustration, irritation and anger are natural feelings. They are caused by outside occurrences, situations beyond my control, and other people."

These emotions are caused by your own thinking and beliefs. Here is proof: No matter what situation makes you mad, you can find people who would not become upset in this situation. It is *your reaction* that makes the difference.

- "Other people and circumstances are to blame for my negative feelings."

No one is "to blame." Blaming others is an attempt to avoid doing anything constructive about the problem.

- "People ought to agree with me and help me more."

People do what they are caused to do by their own internal processes, not by what you think they ought to do.

- "The world is against me."

The world does not care about you one way or the other; it is neither for nor against you.

- "I should be able to change the world and its people quickly and easily."

You cannot. It takes time, effort, planning, ability, persistence and luck.

- "People should act as I want."

They will act as they want.

- "I should be able to have my way most of the time."

As long as you live or work with others, you must compromise.

- "People who oppose me are bad."

From their point of view, you are probably bad.

- "Nothing will go wrong. All problems can be solved."

We often act as if we believed this. We plan without making allowance for what might go wrong. We convince ourselves that achievement of some goal will make us eternally happy. The reality of life is the opposite: something can always go wrong, and often does. There will always be problems to be solved.

- "I can do anything if I really want to."

This is a popular maxim from the "Positive Thinking Can Do Anything" school of thought, but it is false. There are many things you cannot do, considering both your circumstances and your abilities. Recognize that you have limitations. Act in ways that will maximize your chances for success and happiness. Do not pursue hopeless goals.

In sum: Accept the world for what it is. Avoid beliefs based solely on wishful thinking and self-deception.

3. Achieving Emotional Control

By learning to control your thoughts, you can learn to control your emotions. Here are some specific guidelines:

- Decide that you are going to avoid all useless frustration, irritation and anger. Form workable plans for doing so.

Instead of letting yourself become angry, make yourself think of a plan for solving the problems or, at least, making the best of the situation. Make yourself act in a constructive way, even if you do not feel like it. (Remind yourself: getting angry is stupid.)

- Think in ways that have beneficial results.

Deliberately give up thoughts that cause you to become upset. Do not dwell upon disappointments; this just makes you feel sorry for yourself. Give little thought to unimportant things. Do not allow what is merely *urgent* to crowd out what is truly *important*. When you are annoyed by some characteristic of another person, find a way to alter your feelings. Think about his good features, for example. Do the same for any annoying situation. Do not just sit there thinking, "Isn't this awful!" Either change the situation, or change your reaction to it.

- Consider other people. Think about subjects other than yourself and what you want.

Try to gain a broader perspective. Make yourself useful. Regard other people as potential friends, even if they seem to be acting against you. Do not give way to anger, even if you feel justified in doing so. Keep thinking about ways to maximize long-range benefits for all.

• Do not give up.

Emotional habits of a lifetime are not broken in a day or two. Continue the effort until you achieve the results you want.

4. Preserving Useful and Appropriate Reactions

If you were *completely* successful in eliminating frustration, irritation and anger, you would become a freak, an unnatural human being. It is both appropriate and desirable to experience these feelings under certain conditions.

For instance, in the presence of an outrageous crime or cruelty, such as murder or child abuse, you *should* feel strong emotion. Even police officers, who face these situations daily, are not expected to become wooden statues. Lack of any feeling would indicate an individual who is not functioning properly.

None the less, police officers, and all of us, are still expected to control our actions. We are expected to act in ways that have the best results under the circumstances. We are supposed to do our duty, even if we feel like doing something else. Therefore, do not think that you should or will be excused if you let strong emotion cause you to do something wrong.

Frustration can be good if it makes you work harder to solve your problems. When it leads you to defend yourself in dangerous situations, anger is good. Irritation is useful if it motivates you to take corrective action.

Do not try to prevent yourself from reacting as a

normal human being, feeling normal emotions in stress-ful situations. Instead, learn to recognize when your feelings are not appropriate for the circumstances or are too destructive. Gain control of these feelings, so you can act in ways that have the best overall effect.

SUMMARY

Frustration, irritation and anger are emotions caused by our beliefs, which are themselves caused by failure to expect problems and/or inability to solve them. To avoid these emotions, eliminate false and unrealistic beliefs, make yourself think constructively, and think of problems to be solved and of other people besides your-self. Learn to control your emotions when they become unreasonable, but do not try to eliminate all normal human reactions.

APPLICATIONS

1. Make a list of common events that make you angry. Include any of the following which bother you strongly.

Other drivers.

Being told what to do.

Trying and continually failing.

Not making progress.

Party games.

Waiting in a doctor's office, theater line, restaurant, etc.

Your wife (husband).

People who are ungrateful.

Violence, cruelty or intolerance.

Underdone food.

People who talk too much.

Your in-laws.

The evening news.

The Boss.

A highly-promoted product that turns out to be no good.

Stairs.

Nothing to do.

Your parents.

Yourself.

Liars.

People who back out of a commitment.

Waiting for others to do something.

Being gypped (cheated).

Child neglect or abuse.

Disobedience, insubordination or disloyalty.

The I.R.S.

People who are ungenerous.

Blasphemy, sacrilege or obscenity.

Noise.

Idiots.

Your daughter's boyfriend.

The neighbor's dog.

Your unreliable, expensive-to-fix old car.

Small print.

Urban sprawl or pollution.

Too much to do.

Your children.

Etc.

For each irritant you have listed, decide whether you will correct the problem by (1) taking positive action to change what is bothering you, or (2) taking positive action to change your emotional reaction to it.

For instance, there will always be people who drive

irresponsibly or in ways that annoy you. If you allow yourself to become upset with them, your own driving will be less safe, which could result in an accident. Your best decision is to control your reactions to them. (A "Defensive Driving" course teaches some methods for doing this.)

On the other hand, anger at being cheated could be good. It could impel you to a course of action which would result in your recovering your money, or would prevent the perpetrators from victimizing someone else.

2. Teach others these methods for avoiding anger. Use them to solve frustration and anger problems among your employees or co-workers. Combine this chapter with the principles of correcting faults in others.

EXAMPLES

1. "I have a high-pressure job which is causing me a lot of stress. I cannot yell at my customers or tell-off the boss, but I cannot keep going like this either. What can I do?" **What is your answer?**

Discussion: In some cases, learning relaxation methods could solve the problem or reduce it enough for the person to continue. In other cases, resigning from the job and taking up a less-stressful career may be the best answer. The final decision must rest with the individual.

Here are some practices which may help:

- Getting more exercise (This is relaxing in itself and it promotes health, which will help the person handle his stressful position);

- Using frustration-releasers, such as meditation, reading, or running around the block when the tension becomes too intense;
- Avoiding dependence on stimulants and depressives such as alcohol and drugs (These have a rebound effect, making the original condition worse when they wear off, and an addictive effect, requiring ever-increasing doses to achieve the same results);
- Gaining greater control over the work situation, which has been shown to create a better sense of well-being and a decrease in dysfunctional responses;
- Adopting a belief system or thought-control method which will modify those beliefs now causing distress (through religion, meditation, positive thinking, self-acceptance, etc.).

If none of these methods help enough, the person should seek professional help. Many employers provide stress counseling through their Employee Assistance Programs.

2. "I feel trapped. I can never escape from my children, my spouse, my in-laws, my boss, my job, my house, or my oppressive routine. I have no control over my life at all. My reactions seem to belong to someone else. The only time I am free is in my daydreams, where nobody can get at me. I often feel that life is just not worth living. What can I do?"
What is your answer?

Discussion: This person should get professional counseling, as soon as possible. There are some emotional problems that *no one* can handle alone. If you know of anyone like this person, or are this person, do not delay. Do not think that the problems will go away by themselves. Do not think that the person is just "faking it." Emotional problems *can* get out of control. *Get help!*

CHAPTER 19

AVOIDING TENSION, DISCOURAGEMENT AND FATIGUE

The Problem

Stress induces physical, psychological and behavioral distress. Some researchers have suggested that fifty percent or more of complaints brought to medical doctors are psychogenic, that is, brought on by stress and other psychological factors. Stress can cause career burn-out, dependence on addictive substances, interpersonal conflicts, a negative self-image, susceptibility to disease, and generally poor personal performance.

Release from stress can free you to achieve more (you will no longer be dragged down by fatigue and discouragement), make and keep friends (no one wants to be around a tired, tense negative-thinker) and feel better about yourself. As you eliminate negative beliefs about yourself, accomplish more and are of greater help to others, you will have good reason to feel better.

Causes

Tension, discouragement and fatigue are like frustration, irritation and anger in this way: they are all negative emotions which can rob you of happiness and diminish your effectiveness. A major difference between these feelings lies in their results. Tension, discouragement and fatigue are passive emotions: they make you feel like quitting, giving up, and doing nothing. Frustration, irritation and anger are active emotions: they make you feel like doing something, such as attacking whatever is bothering you.

Tension is produced by the belief that something may not turn out as you want or by dissatisfaction with how things are going. Tension occurs when you hold yourself in readiness to respond but you cannot act because of the circumstances. An example is driving through fog. You are ready to react to anything in the road ahead, but you cannot do so unless and until an obstacle appears. This holding-yourself-in-readiness produces the tension.

Beliefs which commonly cause tension are

- "I am in danger";
- "I must be careful";
- "I must make the right decision and do the right thing."

Discouragement is caused by believing, "I cannot do it." It comes from trying and failing or knowing of no way to succeed. It is common when you are tired and have no energy left to solve your problems.

Tension combined with discouragement produces fatigue. (We are not talking about purely physical fatigue from exercise.) The mental tension of holding important concerns in your thoughts creates a psychological tiredness. Psychological tension causes you to tense your muscles, especially in the neck and back. After a period of time, this leads to physical weariness.

The natural result is that you feel tired. Now, however, you have an additional problem. Before, you had worries. Now you have the same worries, but have no energy left to solve them. This leads to even more stress, which causes more fatigue, which causes more discouragement.

If unchecked, this self-reinforcing spiral of stress, fatigue and discouragement could result in a psychological breakdown. Hospitalization and therapy might be required to overcome it.

Possible Solutions

1. Use Positive Thinking to Eliminate False and Useless Beliefs

"Positive Thinking" means deliberately thinking about the positive aspects of a situation instead of the negative ones, and being optimistic instead of pessimistic. It also means assuming that you can do something, instead of cannot.

Positive thinking works because it removes the thoughts and opinions that are producing your fear, anxiety, tension and discouragement. Thinking about the good features of a situation causes appropriate positive emotions. Thinking, "I can do it," instead of, "I will fail," replaces discouragement with optimism.

One of the most valuable functions of positive thinking is removal of false and unwarranted opinions. These usually spring from habit or fear, rather than a realistic evaluation of the situation.

Here are some of the false beliefs which cause people unnecessary agony. Each can be eliminated by thinking positively instead of negatively.

- "I do not like my job."

If you are going to do it anyway, you might as well enjoy it. *Decide* to enjoy it.

- "I have to associate with her, but I do not like her."

If you have to associate with her, why not try to like her? Find things about her that you do like and concentrate on those. Find a pleasant way to interact. Ignore or change your attitude toward whatever it is that annoys you.

- "I do not want to do this, but I have to."

When you say that you "have to" do something, you usually mean that you are doing it because of its results, which you do want. In some imaginary and perfect world, it might be possible to achieve the results you want by doing only actions you enjoy. Unfortunately, that is *not* true of this world. We freely choose to do disagreeable tasks because they are worth it to us for the results they bring. Therefore, when you do what you "have to do," you are really doing what you have freely chosen to do. All things considered, in the world as it is, this is the best choice open to you. Instead of making yourself unhappy by thinking, "I have to do this," say to yourself, "I want to do this because of the wonderful things it will bring me."

- "I cannot get what I want."

Say instead, "I have not yet found a way to get what I want."

- "I cannot do this task."

If you have good evidence for your opinion, such as having tried repeatedly and failed badly, then your belief is realistic and should be accepted. However, if you have not tried it or have not tried your best, or the results are not yet known, then the opinion is unfounded. Reject it in favor of the more optimistic one, "I might be able to do this."

- "I am not going to realize my life goals."

Again, examine the evidence to see if it is definitely established that you will fall short of your goals. If the evidence is not conclusive, choose the optimistic alternative of believing that you may achieve them. On the other hand, if there is good evidence that you will not achieve your goals, change them. Discard your old objectives and enthusiastically adopt new ones. Everyone gives up goals. We do so to devote the necessary effort to achieving the ones we want more. Sometimes, of course, you will fail. The only serious mistake you can make then is continuing to pursue hopeless dreams. Put aside these former hopes; put them out of your mind. Pursue your new goals with uninhibited commitment and enthusiasm.

- "I am not getting anywhere."

This belief usually indicates lack of a clear objective. If you have a goal, you can measure progress toward or away from it. If you do not have a goal, you can never have any feeling of progress. In some cases, you may have chosen an impossible goal, toward which progress would never be significant. Do not torture yourself for not achieving the impossible. Find other goals. Keep a record to measure your progress. Use it to show yourself that you are advancing, that you can achieve your objectives, and that your plans and actions are effective. You will then *feel* that you are making progress because you will *know* you are.

• "I should not have to work so hard."

Aside from luck, work is the only way to get what you want. Anything worthwhile requires it. It is the source of true satisfaction. Decide to enjoy your work, or find other work that you do enjoy. Decide that you "deserve" exactly as much as you can achieve, regardless of what others may do or have.

• "I have more than my share of difficulties."

Difficulties are no fun, but they do provide some surprising benefits. For one thing, great achievement is possible only if there is some great problem to be overcome. Many of the world's outstanding individuals accomplished what they did in the face of enormous obstacles. Perhaps this was what made them great.

Problems provide these other advantages: (1) they provide the opportunity to show what you can do; (2) they develop your abilities; (3) they make life interesting; (4) they motivate you; (5) they produce a feeling of genuine satisfaction when they are overcome; (6) they attract the help and admiration of others. Most of the time, when you think about how difficult your problems are, you are just feeling sorry for yourself. Self-pity is one of the least admirable of human traits. Welcome your share of life's difficulties for the blessings they can be.

• "Other people should help me more."

Other people have their own concerns. For a more satisfying experience in life, decide to solve your own problems. Take responsibility for your own happiness, and help others instead of demanding help from them.

• "I am no good."

We are most apt to think badly of ourselves after suffering a failure or setback. Most of the time, this feeling is only disappointment, plus a bit of feeling sorry for ourselves. To overcome it, think of others instead of yourself, and of problems to be solved. Do not judge yourself on such a narrow basis. Consider the good things you have done in the past and the many worthwhile accomplishments awaiting you in the future.

• "Life is not worth living."

This is true only if you make it true in your own mind. There are probably millions of people who would gladly trade places with you. Figure out what is really troubling you, then get rid of it or solve it. Embrace the positive. Say, "Life is worth living because I have decided that it is; I choose to live happily."

2. Use Positive Action to Change Undesirable Circumstances

Unfortunately, Positive Thinking will not solve all problems. It will not even solve all problems of negative thinking.

The fact is that a person *cannot* force himself to believe what all of his knowledge and experience tell him is not so. If he can find a fallacy in his previous reasoning, or a possibility of error, then he could use positive thinking to reject a negative conclusion. But if everything points to the truth of that conclusion, no sane person could make himself disbelieve it.

Try this: make yourself believe that you could lift the Sears Tower, or one of the pyramids of Egypt, barehanded. If you can believe this, then you are crazy. You ought to be locked up for your own protection and the safety of the rest of us.

Here are some other beliefs you should have trouble

making yourself believe:

- You can succeed in an area where you have no knowledge, no experience and no ability;
- You can sell obviously-defective merchandise to the shrewdest buyers in the business;
- You can make a product line profitable again, even though it is obsolete and poorly designed, and competing products are both better and cheaper.

Positive thinking lets us down when we need it the most, that is, when we have every reason to believe that disaster is on our doorstep and there is nothing we can do to stop it. Even if we could make ourselves believe positively in the face of obvious negative facts, we would not help ourselves because we would then make terrible decisions.

What is needed is a realistic assessment of the situation, not wishful thinking. Only by realistic planning can you possibly solve your problems, or at least minimize the damage. Furthermore, failure to acknowledge problems can make you look ridiculous and cause others to lose confidence in your judgment.

This leads us to the concept of *"Positive Action."* It means doing something useful, something that will solve the problems or improve the situation.

If a positive action does not resolve all difficulties, it still helps combat tension, discouragement and fatigue. These are passive emotions, so by taking action you are working against them. The satisfaction which comes from any accomplishment will help to weaken them further.

Another factor will come to your aid when you act positively. Fear and tension are strongest before action, as shown in studies of soldiers before and during combat. Once you get yourself into action, you will generally find that the situation is not as bad as you imagined. In any case, you will then be too busy to worry so much.

Any action which improves the situation will help in diminishing tension, discouragement and fatigue. The action need not affect the problem directly. For example, if you have been struggling with a management puzzle all afternoon, positive action could consist of going to the YMCA for a swim. The exercise and change of scene could make you feel better and able to work effectively again.

These are the steps for taking Positive Action:
1. When positive action is needed, *decide to act now.*

Decide to *do* it. Do not "think about it." If action is important and delay is a danger, get yourself going, even if you might not have considered all the nuances of the situation. Many problems cannot be totally reasoned out ahead of time. Try something, observe the result, then make corrections. Try again till you get it right.
2. Make yourself think productively.

Do not let your mind drift from the main objective. Try to foresee problems. If they do arise, decide what you are going to do as quickly as possible. Then, put that decision into effect immediately.
3. Decide on the right things to do, then keep on doing them until they succeed.

Most plans require a period of time to be effective. This is why many new businesses fail. It takes too long for the actions of their managers to have the needed results. They have run out of start-up capital and must quit before then.

Giving up too soon is a mistake, but so is staying too long in the face of probable failure. You should see progress and indications of future success from an early time.

4. Do not be afraid to do things your way, follow your own lights, and be yourself.

You can never be happy just doing what others want. You must put some of your individuality into your life and work. Do not let your chance for success and happiness pass by because you are afraid to discover and do what is right for you. This does not mean you should abandon your family and career or run away to sea; it does mean actively seeking to make your life meaningful for you.

5. Decide that you will do whatever is necessary to reach your objectives.

Resolve that you will not give up when unexpected obstacles appear, you are weary and discouraged, or others oppose your chosen course. Acquire the needed skills and knowledge. Pay the price in time, money and effort. Overcome setbacks. This is what it takes to achieve anything worth doing and worth having.

If you are not willing to make these sacrifices to reach your goals, it is a good indicator that you do not really want them. Find some objectives you are willing to "suffer for." They are what you really want.

6. Have fun.

Do not wait to enjoy yourself until "someday," when you retire, or your children are grown, or whatever. Why endure a miserable life on the chance that you will have a bit of happiness at its end? That is a poor investment.

You need to take breaks from working to enjoy the benefits you have earned. This reinforces your desire to work by rewarding it. You will return from such breaks refreshed, full of enthusiasm and new ideas. Your productivity will increase, not diminish.

One of the easiest and most effective "motivators" you can introduce into your workplace is an atmosphere of enjoyment and good feeling among the people who work there. This is often accomplished through a pattern of humorous exchange, deliberate tension-relievers and acknowledgement of the value of each person to the group.

Decide to enjoy life. Seek out rewards for yourself. As much as possible, enjoy everything you do.

7. Manage your assets for best returns, just like a business.

Your assets include your time, energy, abilities, material resources, helpers (spouse, relatives, employees, friends, others), opportunities and circumstances. If you obtain less return from these than you think you should, or less than others seem to be deriving from their assets, you will be dissatisfied.

As with any business, your goals must be clearly defined. Develop realistic plans and carry them out with dispatch.

All organizations must devote part of their income to maintaining present operations and part to preparing for future needs. There are accepted methods for determining a judicious balance of these for companies in various industries. Too little investment would show up in a lack of new products. Too much would take away from present production needs.

You can apply these same concepts in deciding how much time and energy to devote to your work and how much should go for enjoyment or doing other things. If you develop an extreme fear of failure or a feeling of "not getting anywhere," it may be an indication that you are spending too much time on present desires and not enough on building for the future. If so, get back to work. Set new goals, enroll in training programs, do more research and development, or institute some project that will payoff in the future. On the other hand, if your feelings are dominated by thoughts such as, "Why do I bother to work so hard?" "I cannot keep up," or "I don't really care anymore," then you are probably investing too much in the future and too little in present enjoyment. It is time to relax, buy a new boat, take a vacation, or otherwise get some immediate rewards.

8. Decide to accept responsibility for your own happiness.

This means deciding to *do something* to achieve the results you want for your life.

SUMMARY

Tension, discouragement and fatigue are potentially serious emotional problems. Combat them by using Positive Thinking to eliminate false and unrealistic attitudes. Use Positive Action to actually improve the situation.

APPLICATIONS

1. Most people have more problems with either the active or the passive negative emotions, depending upon their personalities and motivational makeup. Diagnose yourself. Do you have a greater tendency to become frustrated, irritated and angry (the active emotions), or tense, discouraged and tired (the passive emotions)? Diagnose employees in the same way. Those who are more aggressive will have problems with anger and

frustration. You will have to control their tendencies to overreact. Others, who are more passive, will have to be motivated and encouraged.

2. Read the literature on the connection between stress, behavior and health. Find ways to keep excessive tension from becoming a problem in your own life and in the working conditions of your department. Be aware of its symptoms. If employees feel pressure, then it exists, even if you did not intend to create it. Use methods from this chapter to reduce it.

EXAMPLES

1. Why is Positive Thinking more popular than Positive Action as a self-help method?

(One possible answer: You can do it sitting down, that is, "just thinking" is easier than taking action.)

2. What is the biggest obstacle to going your own way and doing things as you want?

(One possible answer: Fear.)

3. Why do some people want to eliminate all fun from their lives and do "serious" work all the time?

(One possible answer: They think enjoyment is evil, or are overly afraid of failure.)

4. Have you decided to accept full responsibility for your success and happiness, including all of your emotional reactions?

(Two possible answers: 1. "Yes. By accepting responsibility, I have the best chance of success." 2. "No. I cannot take responsibility for every problem. That would mean I would have to do something about everything. This is more stress than I can handle." Each answer is sensible. Yours will depend on your personality and philosophy of life.)

CHAPTER 20

DEVELOPING A POSITIVE PERSONAL PHILOSOPHY

A Personal Philosophy: Why You Need It

Every group looks to its leader for guidance and inspiration. The leader has to have a method for providing it. That method is found in his personal philosophy and outlook.

Without a philosophy, there would be no good way to make decisions. There would be no organizing principles or a method for selecting goals. There would be no values to use in judging excellence. There could be no sense of self-worth, importance or contribution.

The kind of philosophy needed is an integrated understanding of life, the world, society, the organization, and the place of each individual in the process. It is also a system of values, goals and priorities. A truly satisfying philosophy is satisfying in and of itself, and because it leads to sound decisions.

Guidelines for Developing a Positive Philosophy

For help in leading your department, you should find guidance in your corporation's overall management philosophy. In some companies, this is explicit. In others, it is learned by implication: through training programs and daily experience.

Your personal philosophy is also important. It is important for your success as a leader and for your own satisfaction.

Here are some suggestions for developing you own philosophy of life and work.

1. Identify your most important values and beliefs, keep these central, and act on them.

There should be some principles that are so basic to an organization or individual that no compromise or exception is allowed. Do not be so irresolute, fearful, lazy, well-off or socially insecure that you back away from these. It is important for every person, every leader and every group to have something to count on as core values and standards of behavior.

On the personal level, this means finding the things in your life that are most important to you. When you find these, pursue them over other values and goals. Do not allow your opportunity for true success to escape because you are overly afraid or insufficiently motivated to grasp it.

2. Remember that satisfaction comes from what you do, not from what you passively receive.

When you earn a reward through honest and skilled effort, you feel a contentment and a pride that has no equal. Receiving rewards without this sense of accomplishment is hollow. You think you should be totally happy and wonder why you are not. Besides yourself, everyone in your organization needs to feel this sense of accomplishment. Be sure they have opportunities to do so. People may think they want something for nothing, but you now know better. Plan the work and rewards to produce true satisfaction for all.

3. Select goals that are both worthy in themselves and that have good effects.

There are ways to get ahead by cheating or mistreating others. You can justify this, if you want to, by claiming that many are out to cheat you or just do not care. This may be true. Even so, if *you* think your goals or methods are less than admirable, then you will feel shame rather than pride in what you do.

A wise executive will make sure that organizational methods, as well as its goals, are admirable to all. Employees will not feel like doing their best for an organization that does not do its best.

In your personal life, find goals you both *want to achieve* and *believe to be worthwhile*. You can gain satisfaction from pursuing goals you believe to be worthy, even if you do not reach them, or do not achieve what other people may regard as great success. Remember the character Faust: he gave his soul to the Devil in order to obtain worldly power and riches, and then lost everything. This is an allegory, warning us that we can lose our chance for true success and happiness if we pursue the wrong goals *or* use the wrong methods to achieve them.

4. Regard life as a great adventure.

Like any adventure, life gives us

- an opportunity to gain and a danger of losing, at

every stage;

- outcomes that are determined partly by factors within our control (through our planning and actions) and partly by factors outside our control (circumstances and "luck");
- results that are never known ahead of time.

Indeed, life is *the* great adventure.

Applications to Management

A group looks to its leader for an expression of the organization's philosophy and exemplification of a positive personal code.

You set an example for people in your organization to follow. You influence others by demonstration of your values, goals and beliefs, and by your habits, behavior and even your appearance. Decide what effects you want to have. Act to produce them. *Create* the outlook needed by your group.

As a leader and manager, you have a wonderful opportunity. You can help people perform useful work, benefit others, and gain success for themselves. Working together, you and they can achieve great things.

SUMMARY

A person's philosophy of life guides him, as an organization's philosophy guides it. You convey both to your employees. Select goals that are of value in themselves and that lead to good decisions. Create a positive outlook in your group and provide opportunities for real satisfaction. See life itself for the great adventure that it is.

APPLICATIONS

1. Here is a list of common life goals. Rank them in order of importance to you.
    -   Financial success.
    -   Marriage partner.
    -   Children.
    -   Service to the community.
    -   Vocational satisfaction.
    -   Respect of the community.
    -   Health.
    -   A satisfying philosophy of life.

You can use this list to help clarify your own philosophy.

Do not expect to ever totally finish your personal philosophy. You will want to revise it periodically and carry it forward throughout your life. Also, do not expect to just borrow one from somewhere. You must develop your own, to suit you.

2. Obtain a clear understanding of your organization's philosophy and how it applies to your department. You should know the organization's values, objectives, priorities and procedures.

Corporate philosophy will change as a result of new leadership, internal organizational needs, and the political, social and economic conditions. Part of your job is to keep up to date on such changes, apply them in your area, and interpret them as needed to the people under your supervision.

STEP THREE

MEETING
THE MANAGEMENT
LEADERSHIP CHALLENGE

CHAPTER 21

MANAGEMENT THEORIES AND THE LEADERSHIP CHALLENGE

Step One describes a true leader as one who seeks to help others, as well as himself, by using the methods of mutual assistance. A true leader does not employ force, as an autocratic manager does, or deception, as a manipulative manager would do. He does not *need* to use these methods because people will follow him willingly to achieve something they want. He does not *want* to use these methods because he recognizes their serious negative consequences, including resistance and resentment.

The traditional definition of leadership is "obtaining desired results through the willing efforts of other people." In the traditional view, *resistance from others* is the primary obstacle for a leader to overcome.

Over the years, various management theories have been formulated to show managers how to handle resistance. The "Human Relations" movement emphasized the need for good relationships between supervisors and workers. "Democratic Management," "Quality Circles," and "Teamwork Training" all sought to eliminate the resistance and resentment which employees might feel as a result of status or power differences between them and their managers. More recently, "Devotion to the Organization" and "Sharing in a Vision for the Organization" have been advocated as methods of avoiding resistance and motivating workers to achieve company objectives.

By combining the best features of all these theories, a manager should be able to

- eliminate resistance by treating employees well;
- abolish resentment, by de-emphasizing differences in status and by encouraging feelings of participation and belonging;
- create loyalty and gain cooperation, by developing team spirit and devotion to the organization;
- provide inspiration, through a mission or vision for the group and a place for each person in that vision.

This scenario must have seemed very attractive to many managers. Organizations have devoted great efforts and considerable sums of money in attempting to achieve these results.

Unfortunately, the program has not worked as well as hoped. Part of the reason may be that it conflicts with the basic cultural value of *Individualism,* that is, individual freedom and self-determination.

Americans value individualism very highly. This is shown in many ways.

- Fundamental government documents and political writings speak time and again of the value of the individual and of individual freedom. The basic structure of government and numerous laws passed over the years affirm the national determination to protect individual freedom, encourage individual initiative and provide equal individual opportunity.
- Newspapers, television, movies and literature glorify individuality. Free enterprise is praised and entrepreneurship encouraged. Those who succeed are society's heroes.

Individualism is valued not only for its own sake, but also for its results. It is credited with much of America's success. Individual initiative is part of the reason the United States has led the world in innovation and discovery. In recent years, when some of the largest corporations have been in trouble, individual entrepreneurs have provided new jobs and economic growth. The individual freedoms and responsibility of citizens are what make this democracy work as a form of government.

Americans so highly value their tradition of individualism that they will defend it against *any* organizational values which they perceive as overemphasized. *This attitude creates something of a paradox for managers: the more effectively they overcome resistance, obtain teamwork and generate devotion to organizational goals, the more their actions come into conflict with the individualistic tradition.*

If America was to emulate other societies and their systems, such as the Japanese in their successful manufacturing and trade practices, it would have to adopt the features of those systems that make them work. That could include the routine sacrifice of individual objectives in favor of group goals, unwavering devotion to the organization, and centralized government coordination of industries.

Likewise, if the country sought to increase efficiency by copying the methods of highly authoritarian societies, it would have to accept the extreme respect for authority and blind obedience of orders which are necessary parts of those systems.

Because of America's individualistic tradition, these alternatives are unacceptable. The United States needs a management philosophy that will express its fundamental values, suit its peoples, and emphasize the strengths of its social and economic systems.

The leadership challenge for American managers — and for managers everywhere that individual freedom and initiative are valued — is this:

To achieve organizational goals while *allowing and encouraging* each employee's individual freedom, initiative, creativity, productivity and responsibility.

CHAPTER 22

COOPERATIVE
INDIVIDUALISM

The need to foster cooperation in organizations has always been clear. The encouragement of individualism is equally important, for these reasons.

First, it recognizes the primacy of the individual as agent. All action is really individual action. Group action is just combined individual actions, entirely dependent upon the activity or inactivity of each person in the group.

Second, individual action requires individual motivation. While it is true that people working together can usually accomplish more than lone individuals, any highly directed group activity loses motivation on the personal level. A person's desire to work drops when she lacks significant control over the results. That happens when she is just one of many or is distant from the group leadership. Leaders often attempt to combat this kind of apathy by exerting even greater control, but it just makes matters worse. Ultimately, the group can become entangled in repressive restrictions and bureaucracy. Then, except for the few in charge, no one is committed to productive action.

Third, an emphasis on individual initiative creates greater flexibility. Individuals can usually change direction faster than organizations. In addition, having many innovative people will result in a greater number and variety of initiatives, one of which may be highly successful ("just what is needed") in changing circumstances.

Is a system which values individualism able to compete successfully with more group-centered methods?

Every type of system has its advantages. It is reasonable to expect that individual-centered and group-centered methods would each have advantages for some products and services, at some times and places, and under some conditions.

An individualistic system can compete successfully by taking advantage of those areas where it is superior. For example, it may not be as good for "low-tech" or routine manufacturing, for mass manual labor or for working with uneducated workers who are used to authoritarian rule. It should excel where individual initiative and innovation are the keys to success. That could include creation of new products, development of new business and management methods, a flexible workforce, entrepreneurship, scientific and academic research, higher education, some forms of artistic creation, and the widespread competence of professionals and specialists.

I would like to suggest "Cooperative Individualism" as the name for a management philosophy that values and encourages responsible individualism. The name makes it clear that individualism is the primary concept. It implies the desirability of individual expression in group functions, not just from the leaders but from everyone. Initiative is to be encouraged and rewarded, as is individual responsibility for performance. In return, each person will know that we value him as an individual and that we want him to benefit from his association with us.

By calling our individualism "Cooperative," we are saying that we work together willingly, to achieve common goals. In order to cooperate, we are prepared to set aside some of our individual freedoms, including the unrestricted freedom to act without consulting others. We will agree to fulfill our part of an accepted plan, promote the group goal over any individual ones that may interfere, and obey people in leadership positions as needed for the plan to succeed. On the other hand, we do not give up individual freedoms *except* as required for the mutual effort. We do *not* give up individual expression and preference in seeking ways to achieve the group objective, nor do we give up the right to try to revise the group plan or even withdraw from it if we find that it is no longer "worth it" to us in terms of our own efforts and rewards.

I believe in Cooperative Individualism and have tried to follow it in my own management practices. I am convinced that it works (and works well!). Some of its advantages are that people learn to perform on their own, solve problems for themselves and assume more responsibility. It encourages long-term relationships; everyone is more relaxed and comfortable with each other. The climate created is attractive to people with ability and initiative, because it treats them with respect and provides opportunities for individual action and development.

The methods of this book are consistent with the philosophy of Cooperative Individualism. However, they are not dependent on it. You can use the methods described regardless of what management philosophy you adopt.

Using these methods, you *can* learn to gain cooperation, avoid resistance and resentment, communicate effectively, convince, persuade, "motivate," correct faults and control negative emotions. With these skills, and the right motivation, you should become an outstanding leader.

I wish you *much* success.

INDEX

For more information
or to order additional copies,
see Order Form on next page.

ORDER FORM

Telephone Orders: (219) 462-2181
                         (8:30 - 4:30 weekdays, Central Time)

Postal Orders: Davidson Manors, Inc., Publishers
                         P.O. Box 548
                         Valparaiso, IN 46384

GUARANTEE
You may return undamaged books *for any reason.*
You will receive a full refund of the purchase price.

Please send me the following books:

THE LEADERSHIP WAY (hardcover):
  Number of books_____ @ $24.95 =   _____

Sales Tax: Books sent to Indiana addresses,
              add 5% sales tax.   _____

Shipping: $2.00 for the first book; $1.00 for each
              additional book. (Surface, book rate.)   _____

              For Air Mail, which is much faster,
              the rate is $4.00 per book.   _____

Total Enclosed: _____

Make check to *Davidson Manors, Inc., Publishers*

Ship To:

Name: _____

Company: _____

Address: _____

City:_____ State: _____ Zip: _____

_____   Check here if you would like information on
           seminars, training programs and consulting services.